The Cost of Worship

Melessa A. Brown

Copyright© 2014 by Melessa A. Brown & Chenaniah World Music Publishers.

All rights reserved. All songs copyrighted by Chenaniah World Music Publishers.

No part of this publication may be reproduced, stored in a retrieval system or transmitted in any form or by any means, electronic, mechanical, photocopying, recording or otherwise, without the express written permission of the copyright holder.

Published in the United States of America.

Published and distributed by Chenaniah World Music Publishers, PO Box 590161, Fort Lauderdale, FL 33359.

Email address: Chenaniahworldpub@aol.com
Website address: www.chenaniahministries.com

Printed in the United States of America.

Scripture notations, unless otherwise noted, are from The King James Version of the Bible, copyright© 1979, 1980, 1982, Thompson Chain Reference Bible, Inc. Used by permission.

ISBN: 978-0-692-26179-8

Melessa A. Brown
The Cost of Worship

Special Thanks & Acknowledgements

First, to my Daddy God, who continues to reveal himself to me, more and more each day; Thank you for keeping me on the "backside of the desert" (causing me to die to self!), and for pouring all of your fullness into me. I thank you for both your pressing, and your prodding. I thank you for revealing Worship to me, and for teaching me its importance. Thank you for your unfailing love. Oh, how I love worshiping you!

I would, also, like to graciously thank the following persons:
My father, Frank Brown Jr., who always instilled in me a since of duty, and commitment. He taught me that my word was my "bond". It was from him that I learned to appreciate International Cuisine, and my desire to "see" the world. It was also from him that I inherited my insatiable thirst for History.

Roschnell, Frank III, Jada, and Sybil (my dear siblings), for your prayers, love and support. You've been there since the beginning, encouraging me onward.

My Pastors, Apostles Ed & Yvette Brinson, for your life of integrity and for your support. Thank you for accepting me into the Redeeming Word "family".

My music teachers, Davene Wilson, Jean Gross, Loretta Whitaker, Patricia Barns-Griffith, and Carl Smith, for taking the time to teach me much, much more than music; for you pruned me, shaped me, and gave me "Life" skills.

Mrs. Joyce Hutcherson, who taught me how to lay on my face before the Lord, and how to pray "deliverance for the captives".

John "Johnny Lips" Boyer, and his dear wife Amy, who have always supported and believed in me. Thank you for the hours spent talking about true worship. I thank you for your invaluable friendship.

Elton & Edith Pride, whose ideas and support have been invaluable. Only heaven will reveal how much. Elton, thanks for coaching me, and Edith, thanks for being relentless….until I wrote this book.

Missy (Trish), thanks for your inimitable assistance, and support. I owe you several Crab dinners!

"Global Mother" …Bernadette, my "big" sister, who is consistent in my life as prayer warrior, confident, supporter, administrator, and iron-sharpener. I thank God, that you were the one on "guard duty" the day that I "slipped" away into Eternity; and I thank God, that he used you to "call" me back from the dead, that I might fulfill Purpose.

"I thank God upon every remembrance of you…"

In Memoriam

This book is written in loving memory of one truly amazing women, who defied all of the odds, to raise her children in the "...ways of the Lord". That amazing woman was my mother, Mae Anna Brown. She taught us the importance of cultivating a good and godly character, and taught us the importance of having integrity. She instilled in us that church was not an option. She taught us the importance of paying the Tithe, giving the Offering, and supporting Missions. She also taught us the art of truly "giving ourselves" to another. She faithfully "watched" over her "garden". My mother was, indeed, a Proverbs 31 (verses 10-31) wife and mother. We, her children, truly "...called her blessed". On her headstone, it reads as follows: "She, who loved much, was much loved. Pro 31:10-31" My mother was passionate about everything she did: cooking, baking, canning, sewing, quilting, crocheting, nursing, singing, playing the piano, etc... Because she played the piano and sang, I wanted to play the piano and sing. Thanks, mom, for such a sweet legacy!

In loving memory of my maternal great grandmother, Addie Willis, my maternal grandmother Sedalia Miller, and my paternal grandmother Marie Antoinette Brown, from whom I learned the ways of Holiness by observation and example. I learned from them...that as the old song says, "Serving the Lord, will pay off ...after while!"

In loving memory of my maternal Aunt, Sebelle Bond, whose beautiful music, and godly life, helped to change her family, her church, and her community. Thank you, for the countless hours, chasing the songs of "old", and for your impartation into my life.

In loving memory of my baby brother, John Edward Brown, who was such a great support. He was truly as his name declares...beloved. Known for his smile, he kept one on his face...all the way to glory. I miss you, dear heart!

In loving memory of Mrs. Corine Ray, who (seeing destiny and purpose on my life) took the assignment to give me piano lessons. My father, once when going through a financial crisis, told her that I would have to quit taking lessons, because he couldn't afford to pay any longer. In response, Mrs. Ray replied, "Getting her here, is between **you** & God. However, once you get her here, it's between **me** & God." Thanks, Mrs. Ray.

This book is also written in memory of the true pioneers of praise and worship: Reverend Archie Dennis, a true trail-blazer, who helped make the transition easier, as the Church went from Devotional Service to Praise & Worship. He gave us songs like, "No One Can Touch You Like Jesus Can," and, "This Is The Lord's Church, And Jesus Is Lord." He painstakingly ploughed the ground, teaching congregations the power of Worship. Some called him Husband, Father, Pastor, Apostle, Song-singer, and "The Garbage Man's Son"; but I was privileged to call him…"Friend". Thank you, Archie.

The Queen of the song, Danniebelle Hall. Even through your sickness and pain, you kept teaching us about "Daddy God". How could we ever forget your beautiful smile and passionate love for the Father, as you sang to him, proclaiming, "I'd Rather Have Jesus", "Ose BaBa", "Let Me Have A Dream", "You Must Open The Door", "His Spirit Is Here", and "I go to the Rock". You reminded us that God uses "Ordinary People". You truly taught us how to enter into…and enjoy…the presence of the Lord. Thank you, Danniebelle.

That great "trail blazer" Dottie Rambo, who also made her entrance into the great Christian "Hall of Fame". She gave us great songs, such as "Holy Spirit, Thou Art Welcome", "He Looked Beyond My Fault", We Shall Behold Him", and "The Rose". Through great physical pain, she pressed through to write songs that encouraged us, and glorified Him. Thank you, Dottie.

The one that they called "…a true holy man"…Bishop William Morgan James. An apostle, a bishop, a prophet, a pastor, a spiritual father, and a true visionary. He gave birth to the "Latter Rain", which in turn, opened the door for the great Azusa conferences (Tulsa 1987-2001). Thank you, Bishop James.

One of the finest and godliest men, I've ever known, and one of the greatest theologians, of the 21st Century– His Grace…Arch Bishop Veron Ashe, whose revelation and "sound" teachings, challenged a generation of theologians and God-seekers, to "dig deeper", in order to find the "…unsearchable riches" of Worship. Thank you, Bishop Ashe.

And lastly, I dedicate this book to the memory of all of the other countless, and "nameless" pioneers who never sought the spotlight, but kept working faithfully and diligently…breaking up the fallow ground. Thank you, for tilling the soil (with painstaking care), to teach the BODY of Christ the importance of Worship. You 'fought a good fight', you 'kept the faith', and you 'finished the course' that was set before you. You obeyed God, and have 'obtained a good report'…that you were righteous. And after blazing such a beautiful trail, it is wonderful to know that you are waiting at the end of it…..cheering us on!

The Cost of Worship

Table of Contents

Prelude……………………………………………………………………..ix

Introduction……………………………………………………………...xi

Chapter 1……………. The Importance of Getting Wisdom………………...1

Chapter 2……...………..Varied Roles In The Body…………………….....5

Chapter 3………………….......True Worship…………………………………..9

Chapter 4…………….………Preparing Him A Place…………………….....13

Chapter 5………….…………The Praise of Judah………………………….. 31

Chapter 6……………………....…Praise…………………………………..39

Chapter 7………...………………..Worship………………………………….45

Chapter 8……………….……The Cost of Worship………………………..53

Chapter 9…………The Role of The Congregation In Worship……………....61

Chapter 10…………………….A Royal Priesthood…………………………...69

Epilogue………………………………………………………………….75

Prelude

As I entered into a large auditorium for a church conference in Toledo, Ohio, I felt the presence of the Lord in a way that I had experienced, but few times, prior to this "clandestine" meeting. I had had the privilege of singing the liturgical music of eleven different denominations (including a large Jewish synagogue), and working (as soloist) with some of the greatest symphony orchestras in this nation (and several others). And yet, after soaring to the heights with the masters- Bach, Beethoven, Handel, Durafle, Mozart, Verdi, Monteverdi and others, I was having an experience like none other. I was being led in worship, by a master psalmist, Apostle Melessa Brown. As she touched the keys and brought forth her beautiful, sonorous mezzo voice, I heard music that I had never heard before, and yet the words and melodies seemed both ancient and timeless, as if it had waited for me through eternal moments, to join in. I was enraptured in a heavenly interlude, which has carried me, now, for over a decade.

When we hear music of that nature, what does God expect of us, as member of a congregation? He expects us to join in with an expectation of entering into his presence, within his very throne room. Isaiah chapter 6:1-8 says:

> In the year that king Uzziah died I saw also the Lord sitting upon a throne, high and lifted up, and his train filled the temple. Above it stood the seraphims: each one had six wings; with twain he covered his face, and with twain he covered his feet, and with twain he did fly. And one cried unto another, and said, Holy, holy, holy, is the LORD of hosts: the whole earth is full of his glory. And the posts of the door moved at the voice of him that cried, and the house was filled with smoke. Then said I, Woe is me! for I am undone; because I am a man of unclean lips, and I dwell in the midst of a people of unclean lips: for mine eyes have seen the King, the LORD of hosts. Then flew one of the seraphims unto me, having a live coal in his hand, which he had taken with the tongs from off the altar: And he laid it upon my mouth, and said, Lo, this hath touched thy lips; and thine iniquity is taken away, and thy sin purged. Also I heard the voice of the Lord, saying, Whom shall I send, and who will go for us? Then said I, Here am I; send me.

The prophet, Isaiah, realized something critically important to the Father:

(1) He demands worship
(2) The angels continually worship Him with no attendants of darkness present
(3) When you enter into true worship, you see Him the way He really is, and
(4) When you enter into true worship, you see yourself the way you truly are

Isaiah knew he was unclean, and that his generation needed perpetual cleansing, from the Lord. He knew that he could not do due benevolence to the Father, without the fresh cleansing that comes from entering into the presence of the Father. After bowing down before the Almighty, then and only then, could he hear the reason for such an extraordinary encounter, and that reason was to preach and prophecy the word of the Lord, to Israel.

When, as a congregation, we enter into true worship before our Heavenly King, we create an atmosphere for the corporate blessing of the Lord to fall; we make it possible for miracles to come forth, and we open our spirits to entreat God's word, and His orders, for the hour in which we are living. There is simply no greater way to touch the heart of the Father, corporately or privately, than through praise and worship. Demonic principalities flee from those who enter into worship together. It also draws us closer together, as the family of God, when we enter in worship together. Scientifically, it has been discovered that people who believe in the Lord Jesus Christ, and are worshippers, live longer, are sick less, and are able to stand against the sorrows of life, with strength and fortitude. Worship is the most formidable form of warfare, against our common enemy, Satan, and it has been known to destroy cancer cells, open deaf ears, calm and soothe the tortured mind (restoring sanity), and has even been known to raise the dead!

I pray that you discover, through the pages of this book, that worship is far more than you have ever dreamed, takes precedence over everything else that happens in our corporate worship experience, and is **never** to be used as a filler prior to the word preached, or to be shunned by those who do not desire to praise, before the banquet of the word of God. To miss it in a service is like coming to hear the symphony orchestra perform a great masterpiece…with no conductor! The orchestra can read the music and play on its own, but the timing is off, and eveyone is a soloist. If that is the case, where is the harmony? Or worst, yet, where is the unity? And…can it still be defined as a symphony (something characterized by a harmonious combination of elements), or being on one accord?

Allow the true worship experience to connect you to your family in God and raise you to another place in His kingdom, and please devour the book and relish the moments, when you can have the glorious experience with a true master, like Apostle Melessa Brown.

Apostle Pam Vinnett
Author of This Psychic Prophetic Age

Introduction

> *Before I formed thee in the belly I knew thee; and before thou camest forth out of the womb I sanctified thee, and I ordained thee a prophet unto the nations. (Jer. 1:5)*

As far back as I can remember, music has been a part of my life. My paternal grandmother sang in the Gospel Chorus, at her church. (I can still hear her singing, "The Lord Is Blessing Me, Right Now!") My father sang bass in our church's Senior Choir and Male Chorus. In our home town, he was a featured soloist for large crusades and tent revivals. My mother was a soprano in the Senior Choir, and also played the piano. In fact, when my father first saw my mother, she was on stage singing with a band backing her.

My maternal grandfather, aunts, uncles, siblings, and cousins sang. Some played the piano, and others the organ or guitar. Our family reunions usually consisted of testimonies of the Lord's goodness, preaching, and plenty of music and singing! We really enjoyed our times of worship, together.

I was so enamored with music, when I was four years of age, I was given permission to go sit on the organ stool (next to our church organist), every Sunday, as she played her postlude.

By age five, I was receiving proper piano instruction. By the time I was 6, I was playing for the Children's Choir. By age seven, I began teaching songs to the choir. By age nine, I was not only playing for the choir, but I also traveled with my father, on occasions, accompanying him as he sang. By age ten, I was playing for three churches (two Baptist churches, and one Methodist church) and an all-girls group (made up of cousins and friends!) who traveled to minister at various churches. By age eleven, I had been chosen, as musician, to play and sing for my cousin's entire wedding! And by age twelve, I was in the recording studio.

All through my formative years, God placed people of great wisdom around me, so they could impart, into me, some of their wisdom. They were there to give me counsel and help direct my way. Proverbs 11:14 declares, "Where no counsel is, the people fall: but in the multitude of counselors there is safety." In the Message Bible, the same passage reads, "Without good direction, people lose their way; the more wise counsel you follow, the better your chances." (Thank God, I was headed down the right path!)

During these seminal years, I had visited Pentecostal churches where they "praised" the Lord; but the first time that I observed "pure worship", was at an *Andre Crouch and the Disciples* concert at Murray State University (Murray, KY), in 1974. *Andre Crouch*, along with *The Disciples* (made up of his twin sister Sandra, Danniebelle Hall, Bill Maxwell, Harlan Rogers, Fletch Wiley, and Hadley Hockensmith) ministered marvelously. During the concert, I observed people lifting their hands unto the Lord, with tears streaming down their faces. And long after the song had ended, I noticed that their hands would remain lifted!

I hungered and thirsted to know and experience this form of "pure worship", and that hunger and thirst would not be quenched, until I had. My prayers were soon answered, and I've never been the same since!

In Psalms 22:3 David asserts, "But thou art holy, O thou that inhabitest the praises of Israel." I've heard that one of the Japanese translations of this scripture is this:

> "When we truly praise God, we build a big chair for him to come and sit in." (How appropriate!)

I don't know anyone who knows more about worship than David. 2 Samuel 23:1b says that he was... "the anointed of the God of Jacob, and the sweet psalmist of Israel..."

Paul, speaking to the church at Antioch (Acts 13:15-22), rehearses in their ears a portion of the history of the Israelites. He tells them that when they wanted a king, God raised up Saul and made him king. And when Saul disobeyed God, he removed Saul and... "raised up unto them David to be their king; to whom also he gave testimony, and said, *I have found David the son of Jesse, a man after mine own heart, which shall fulfill all my will*." (Italics mine.)

In order to know the Father's heart and do his bidding, we must come before him in worship. He has given us instructions as to how to do just that. In John 4:23-24, Jesus says to the Samaritan woman:

> *But the hour cometh, and now is, when the true worshipers shall worship the Father in spirit and in truth: for the Father seeketh such to worship him. God is a Spirit: and they that worship him must worship him in spirit and in truth.*

In the late 1970's, "Devotional Service" was transitioning out. In fact, when the great worshipers like Archie Dennis, and Danniebelle Hall began to lead us into the presence of God, there was no label for it. However, "Praise & Worship" was, indeed, making its debut. But it did not come without a fight, for you see...old habits don't die easily!

This is one example:

> I was hired, in the mid 1980's, as Worship Director for a church that started its Sunday service, with "Devotional Service".
>
> As "Praise & Worship" began to rise within the Church, our church continued its Devotional Service, and then "Praise & Worship" would follow. The song selection in these devotional Services would often cause a heaviness to "drape" over the song-service, and rather than "lifting the spirit", these songs would make it feel bogged down.
>
> I had the difficult task of bringing them back…(through the "miry clay"!), and into the presence of God! It was an arduous process, getting them to change their perspective regarding Worship.

As the fresh fires of passion and the momentum of Praise & Worship increases, there will always be a need for new and fresh training materials for Pastors, Psalmists, Minstrels, Singers, Dancers, etc... Being adequately trained helps to bring about balance and stability in our Worship Services.

This book is not exhaustive, by any means, but is simply a concise overview of what it really means to extravagantly worship, the true and living God

I pray that this book will be perused by all who desire to enter into the presence of the Lord. I also pray that it will serve as a manual, aiding you in understanding….The Cost of Worship.

Melessa A. Brown
Chenaniah Ministries
Fort Lauderdale, FL

When you come looking for me, you'll find me. Yes, when you get serious about finding me and want it more than anything else, I'll make sure you won't be disappointed.

(Jer. 29:13-14 MSG Bible)

Chapter 1
The Importance of Getting Wisdom

...to know wisdom and instruction; to perceive the words of understanding. (Pro 1:1-2)

In order to understand Worship, you must first get wisdom.

Let's first lay a foundation with some definitions:

- Wisdom- understanding, insight, perception, acumen (expertise), intelligence, astuteness (good judgment), perspicacity (sharpness), shrewdness (prudence)

- Knowledge- Information, skill, data, know-how, comprehension, experience, awareness, understanding, realization, acquaintance, facts

- Understanding- appreciation, grasp, discernment, perception, conception, insight, awareness, knowledge, discretion, tolerance

- Instruction- teaching, training, education, coaching, tutoring, command, direction, tuition, warning, reproof, restraint, rebuke, order, discipline, chastisement (schooling, guidance)

Here's what the opening scripture says in Proverbs 1:1-9 (MKJ Bible):

> The proverbs of Solomon the son of David, king of Israel; to know *wisdom* and *instruction*; to recognize the words of *understanding*; to receive the *instruction* of *wisdom*, justice, and judgment, and uprightness; to give sense to the simple, *knowledge* and judgment to the young man; the wise hears and increases learning; and *understanding* ones get *wisdom*; to *understand* a proverb and its meaning; the words of the wise, and their acute sayings. The fear of Jehovah *is* the beginning of *knowledge*; but fools despise *wisdom* and *instruction*. My son, hear the *instruction* of your father, and forsake not the law of your mother; for they *shall be* an ornament of grace to your head and chains around your neck. (Italics mine)

Now, listen to the same scripture reference, from the Message Bible:

> *These are the wise sayings of Solomon, David's son, Israel's king-- written down so we'll know how to live well and right, to understand what life means and where it's going; A manual for living, for learning what's right and just and fair; To teach the inexperienced the ropes and give our young people a grasp on reality. There's something*

here also for seasoned men and women, still a thing or two for the experienced to learn-- Fresh wisdom to probe and penetrate, the rhymes and reasons of wise men and women. Start with GOD--the first step in learning is bowing down to GOD; only fools thumb their noses at such wisdom and learning. Pay close attention, friend, to what your father tells you; never forget what you learned at your mother's knee. Wear their counsel like flowers in your hair, like rings on your fingers.

So, Solomon is saying that words of wisdom, knowledge, and understanding are given to us so we will have a manual (instruction booklet, or guide book) for learning. As well as being for the inexperienced, this instruction booklet (or guide book) can also teach the experienced some more things. Therefore, we can surmise that increasing in knowledge is perpetual…ongoing. Proverbs 18:15 says, "Wise men and women are always learning, always listening for fresh insights." (MSG Bible)

Let me say this my way. We are tutored (instruction). And as we grasp, appreciate, and begin to discern it (understanding), it turns into skill, know-how, information and experience (knowledge). However, in order to rightly apply this knowledge, we need good judgment, expertise, insight and sharpness (wisdom). [Whew! That was a mouthful!]

A wise journeyman would never begin a journey, without first conferring with a map for instructions or directions as to how to get to his destination. And a wise builder would never begin to build a building, without some type of plan or instruction.

Some musicians think that talent is the most important thing. Others think that it is the only thing. But talent is only a natural ability to do a "thing". It, in itself, has no governing power to help regulate, direct, restrain, or perfect you. For that, you need instruction.

Solomon says that the very first step in learning is 'bowing down to God.' The Modern King James says that the "fear of Jehovah is the beginning of knowledge."

The word *fear* is the Hebrew word *yir'ah* (pron. yir-aw´), and it means to reverence, respect, admire, stand in awe of, and worship.

We will never get off of first base, unless we totally submit to God, reverencing him. We must respect the fact that he is God. We must stand in awe of his excellence, his greatness, his majesty, his omnipotence, his omnificence, his omniscience, and his omnipresence. He is greater than us, and so the lesser must submit to and reverence the greater.

The Message Bible says this in Proverbs 8:10-12:
> *Prefer my life-disciplines over chasing after money, and God-knowledge over a lucrative career. For Wisdom is better than all the trappings of wealth; nothing you could wish for holds a candle to her.*

Let's look at a few more scriptures here.

Proverbs 23:12 says, "Apply thine heart unto instruction, and thine ears to the words of knowledge." The Message Bible interprets the same scripture, this way: "Give yourselves to disciplined instruction; open your ears to tested knowledge." The Contemporary English version articulates it, this way: "Listen to instruction and do your best to learn."

Proverbs 12:1 (MSG) declares, "If you love learning, you love the discipline that goes with it-- how shortsighted to refuse correction!"

In Proverbs 1:7b, Solomon avows that "...fools despise wisdom and instruction." In verse 22, he says that… "they hate knowledge." And Proverbs 19:27, he says, "My son, cease to hear the discipline, only to stray from the words of knowledge."

Let's look at another scripture. It is 2 Timothy 3:16-17:
> *All scripture is given by inspiration of God, and is profitable for doctrine, for reproof, for correction, for instruction in righteousness: That the man of God may be perfect, throughly furnished unto all good works.*

The Greek word for *furnished* is *exartizo* (pron. ex-ar-tid'-zo), and it means to fully equip, or fully supply, for the task ahead.

Let me say it this way:
> All scripture is God inspired, and is advantageous for teaching (or learning), and for critique, straightening up, chastisement, nurturing, and justification; Why? So that you may be complete, and fully equipped.

In other words, God always wants you to succeed. He gives you everything that you need, so that you can accomplish your task.

The same scripture in the Message Bible reads:

Every part of Scripture is God-breathed and useful one way or another--showing us truth, exposing our rebellion, correcting our mistakes, training us to live God's way. Through the Word we are put together and shaped up for the tasks God has for us.

Let's look at one more scripture. It is Ephesians 4:11-13:

And he gave some, apostles; and some, prophets; and some, evangelists; and some, pastors and teachers; For the perfecting of the saints, for the work of the ministry, for the edifying of the body of Christ: Till we all come in the unity of the faith, and of the knowledge of the Son of God, unto a perfect man, unto the measure of the stature of the fullness of Christ:

Now, in the Message Bible:

He handed out gifts of apostle, prophet, evangelist, and pastor-teacher to train Christians in skilled servant work, working within Christ's body, the church, until we're all moving rhythmically and easily with each other, efficient and graceful in response to God's Son, fully mature adults, fully developed within and without, fully alive like Christ.

You may ask, "How long should we receive instruction?" The answer is... it is an ongoing process....until we fully mature (complete, developed, established, full-grown, experienced, responsible). ■

Chapter 2
Varied Roles In The BODY

..the whole body fitly joined together and compacted by that which every joint supplieth (Eph 4:16a)

ROLES: jobs, tasks, occupations, posts, watches, position, profession, function, responsibility, part, trade, skill, employment, craft

Roles are as varied in the Body of Christ as they are in the world. We all have jobs to do, and we must all work. Why? Because, as Paul instructed the church at Thessalonica (2 The 3:10), he gave them this charge: "…if any would not work, neither should he eat."

One Hebrew word for *role* is *choq* (pron. khoke), and it means an enactment, or an appointment, measured by time, space, quantity, labor, and usage. There is another word, and it is *abodah*, (pron. ab-o-daw'), and it means work, assignment, office, labor, service, or ministry. It also means to till the soil. Both of these words infer a task, or an assignment, that will be defined by time, space, quantity, labor, usage, and ministry. The inference, here, is that of tending a job to its completion.

Each of us, has his appointment. We are each assigned different jobs, but each job is important.

Take for instance, General Motors. Its main job designation is called an Assembly Line. On this Assembly Line, each person has a single job to do. One puts on the car's body, another the motor, another the wheels, another the hood, another the trunk, another the headlights, another the hub caps, another the crank shaft, another the fuel line, another the radiator, another the upper heater hose, another the lower heater hose, another the alternator, another the fuel pump, another the fan, another the alternator belt, another the exhaust pipe, another the breaks, another the break another the pads, another the rotors, another the electrical units (which replaced the old distributor caps, points and plugs), another the nuts, another the bolts, another the seats, another the covers, another the roof, another the interior lights, another the stirring wheel, another the speedometer, and still another the thermostat, etc… I'm sure that I'm missing some things. But you follow me, don't you? Good.

Now, if one part is missing…even down to one nut or one bolt, the car won't be complete or whole, and will undoubtedly not live up to the buyer's expectations. It is highly probable that it break down somewhere along the way.

Why? The reason is simple. Each part is significant. Each part that might seem to be insignificant, actually plays a major role in the full running of the vehicle. Would you want to be in that incomplete car? Would you like to get on the highway in it...with its "faulty" breaks, stirring wheel, engine, or thermostat? Would you want to spend hours stranded on the highway in that "lemon" of a car? I'm sure you wouldn't.

Well, the Church is just like that General Motors assembly line. We each have a job to do, in the Body of Christ. Each job is specific, and each job that might seem insignificant to you, is in actuality, just as important as the next.

Ephesians 4:16 and 21 says it so aptly:

From whom the whole body fitly joined together and compacted by that which every joint supplieth, according to the effectual working in the measure of every part, maketh increase of the body unto the edifying of itself in love...In whom all the building fitly framed together groweth unto an holy temple in the Lord...

Let's look at this same verse in the Amplified Bible to better understand:

For because of Him the whole body (the church, in all its various parts), closely joined and firmly knit together by the joints and ligaments with which it is supplied, when each part [*with power adapted to its need*] is working properly [*in all its functions*], grows to full maturity, building itself up in love.

Within the Church's job designations, some are pastors, some are musicians, some are singers, some are elders, some are deacons, some are teachers, some are evangelists, some are missionaries, some are janitors, some are receptionists, some are secretaries, some are greeters, some are armor bearers, some are builders, some are engineers, some are altar workers, some are cooks, and some work in the sound booth. These are only a few of the many functions! But if one part is missing, even down to the janitor cleaning the restrooms, or the lights being turned on, or the sound being turned on, or a teacher not showing up for children's Bible class, or the musician being late for service, the Church won't be complete or whole, and will not live up to God's expectations, or desired plan. It **will** break down, somewhere along the way. Why? The reason, again, is simple. Each job is specific, and each part that might seem to be insignificant in and of itself, plays a major role in the full running of the Church.

Would you want to be in that incomplete church? You know, the church with dirty restrooms and gum stuck on the underside of the pews; or dirty nasty floors, with bugs crawling, and rats running around?

How about that church, where there is no greeter present to welcome you, when you arrive for the very first time? Or maybe the church that has no receptionist available to answer your emergency phone calls, or no elders there to help pray you "through". Would you want to be in a church where an inadequate pastor leaves you hungry all the time, because he cannot give you proper "spiritual" nourishment, and always gives you stale "bread"?!?

When you need a worship atmosphere, so that you can commune with God and get direction, would you want to be in a church where the musician calls in because he has overslept…due to the fact that he has stayed out late Saturday night, partying? **God forbid!!!** I would run far from that church!

Just as there are different roles for each individual in the Body, there are varied roles for us in Worship. Some of you might be psalmists, musicians, singers, dancers, signers, mimes, banner carriers, in drama, or in sound. Whatever our job function, I believe that God gives us grace to fulfill it.

In the book of Nehemiah, we find the story of the Jews returning from exile (Babylon to Jerusalem). Under Nehemiah's leadership, they had 3 main goals: (1) rebuild the wall that was broken down, (2) rebuild the gates that had been burned down, and (3) rebuild the temple and altar that had been destroyed.

Some were assigned to repair the gates, some were to repair the tower of the furnaces, some were to repair the wall of the pool of Siloah, some were to repair the stairs that went down into the city, and some were to repair the walls in between the gates. Others were to repair the temple, and others were assigned to repair the altar. Each person had a job to do.

The rebuilding project took 22 years. The people could have surely given up, but Nehemiah reminded them that the hand of his God was upon him. As he recaps the story (Neh 4:6), he states:

So built we the wall; and all the wall was joined together unto the half thereof: for the people had a mind to work.

The Hebrew word for *mind* is *leb* (pron. labe), and refers to the heart, the will, the intellect, and the stamina (or staying power) to do the work and to see it to its completion.

In the Amplified Bible, Colossians 3:23 reminds us that "whatever may be your task, work at it heartily (from the soul) as [*something done*] for the Lord, and not for men…"

I wrote this little chorus in the late 70's, and it went something like this:

> **Come, Let's Work Together**
>
> Come, let's work together; let's join in one accord
> With one mind and purpose, we're working for the Lord
> Let's have all things in common...
> T'ward the goal we're working for
> Come, let's work together; we're working for the Lord

No matter what our job function is, we are all working toward a common goal.

Remember in Chapter 1, the scripture we quoted from 2 Timothy 3:16-17? It is worth repeating:

All scripture is given by inspiration of God, and is profitable for doctrine, for reproof, for correction, for instruction in righteousness: That the man of God may be perfect, throughly furnished unto all good works.

Remember the Hebrew word for *furnished* (*exartizo*- to fully equip or fully supply for the task ahead)? Don't forget that God always wants you to succeed, and he will give you everything you need, so that you may achieve your goal and complete your task.

The same scripture in the Message Bible reads:

Every part of Scripture is God-breathed and useful one way or another--showing us truth, exposing our rebellion, correcting our mistakes, training us to live God's way. Through the Word we are put together and shaped up for the tasks God has for us.

Paul, speaking to the church at Colossi...encouraging their labor, places emphasis on motive (Col 3:23-24 AMP):

Whatever may be your task, work at it Knowing [*with all certainty*] that it is from the Lord [*and not from men*] that you will receive the inheritance which is your [*real*] reward. [*The One Whom*] you are actually serving [*is*] the Lord Christ (the Messiah).

Let's end this chapter, with a word of encouragement (1Cor 15:58 AMP):

Therefore, my beloved brethren, be firm (steadfast), immovable, always abounding in the work of the Lord [*always being superior, excelling, doing more than enough in the service of the Lord*], knowing and being continually aware that your labor in the Lord is not futile [*it is never wasted or to no purpose*]. ■

Chapter 3
True Worship

But the hour cometh, and now is, when the true worshippers shall worship the Father in spirit and in truth: for the Father seeketh such to worship him. (John 4:23)

The Catholic Creed declares, "The Chief end of man is to glorify God, and enjoy him (adore him, or worship him) forever."

In Isaiah 46:9-10 & 13, God, himself, declares the following:

Remember the former things of old: for I am God, and there is none else; I am God, and there is none like me, Declaring the end from the beginning, and from ancient times the things that are not yet done, saying, My counsel shall stand, and I will do all my pleasure:

I bring near my righteousness; it shall not be far off, and my salvation shall not tarry: and I will place salvation in Zion for Israel my glory.

God doesn't look at things, the way man looks at things. Man always sees the beginning of a thing, and then goes toward its hopeful end. God always sees the end (or the finish) of a thing first, and then begins and completes what He has already seen and purposed to accomplish.

For example, a builder looks at a big billboard or at a miniature model, which is the finished design of a building, and then takes the plans (or drafts) he has made, and works toward the completion of what he has seen.

If our chief end is to worship, then that is our finish (or our goal). Therefore, we should back up to the beginning, and with that same plan (or finish) in mind, build (or work) toward the completion of that chief end.

The Old Testament was originally written in Hebrew. (There where a few chapters in the prophecies of Ezra and Daniel, and one verse in Jeremiah, written in the Aramaic language.) The New Testament was written in Greek. Somewhere in the translation of these languages into the English, much of the original meaning was lost. So, in order to better understand the scriptures, we need to decipher the original languages.

God placed great importance on worship in the Old Testament. He went into great detail, on why it was to take place, how it was to take place, where it was to take place, and when it was to take place. He even placed great detail, on what the priest (and all who served the temple) should wear, what they should sacrifice to him, and how they should prepare these sacrifices that they were to offer up to him.

I'm of this persuasion: If all of this was important to God, then it should be important to us.

The book of John (Chapter 4) begins with Jesus leaving the land of Judea where his disciples had baptized many believers. He then departs unto Galilee, but in order to get there, he must conveniently pass through Samaria.

Let's continue on with the story, beginning at verse 5 (MSG):

> *He came into Sychar, a Samaritan village that bordered the field Jacob had given his son Joseph. Jacob's well was still there. Jesus, worn out by the trip, sat down at the well. It was noon. A woman, a Samaritan, came to draw water. Jesus said, "Would you give me a drink of water?" (His disciples had gone to the village to buy food for lunch.) The Samaritan woman, taken aback, asked, "How come you, a Jew, are asking me, a Samaritan woman, for a drink?" (Jews in those days wouldn't be caught dead talking to Samaritans.)*

Let's stop here a moment, for a little background, on Samaritans.

Before his death, Jacob had blessed all of his sons. To his son, Joseph, his prophetic blessing declared that he was a "...fruitful bough by a well." A *bough* is a son or a builder of the family name. A *well* is a fountain, source, or supply.

This prophetic word was partially fulfilled when Joseph (who had been sold into slavery) preserved his family from extinction (rebuilding their name and being their "source" or supply), during one of the greatest famines, in the land of Egypt. It was further fulfilled in his sons Ephraim (which means *to cause to forget*) and Manasseh (which means *double fruit*) when they inherited the parcel of fertile land that eventually became Samaria (or *Shomeron*, which means *watch tower*).

Later, during the days of Rehoboam (king of Judah), Israel was divided into two kingdoms. The northern kingdom, called Israel, established its capital, first, at Shechem (a revered site in Jewish history) and later at the hilltop city of Samaria.

In 722 B.C., Assyria conquered Israel and took most of its people into captivity. The invaders then brought in Gentile colonists "from Babylon, Cuthah, Ava, Hamath, and from Sepharvaim" (2 Kin. 17:24) to resettle the land.

The foreigners had brought their pagan idols with them. Intermarriage, with these foreigners took place, and the result was Samaritans (or half-breeds).

Soon after resettling, Jeroboam (king of Israel) changed their worship practices (1 Kings 12:25-33), setting up idols in Dan and Bethel. This was done, so that his Jewish citizens would have no need to journey south to Jerusalem in order to offer sacrifices. The resettled Jews, began to worship these pagan idols, alongside the God of Israel (2 Kin. 17:29-41).

The southern kingdom (Israel) was also taking into captivity, but had not intermarried with the Gentile foreigners, as the northern kingdom had done.

Now, back to our story (John 4:5-24):

Jesus answered, "If you knew the generosity of God and who I am, you would be asking me for a drink, and I would give you fresh, living water."

The woman said, "Sir, you don't even have a bucket to draw with, and this well is deep. So how are you going to get this 'living water'? Are you a better man than our ancestor Jacob, who dug this well and drank from it, he and his sons and livestock, and passed it down to us?"

Jesus said, "Everyone who drinks this water will get thirsty again and again. Anyone who drinks the water I give will never thirst--not ever. The water I give will be an artesian spring within, gushing fountains of endless life."

The woman said, "Sir, give me this water so I won't ever get thirsty, won't ever have to come back to this well again!"

He said, "Go call your husband and then come back." "I have no husband," she said. "That's nicely put: 'I have no husband.' You've had five husbands, and the man you're living with now isn't even your husband. You spoke the truth there, sure enough."

"Oh, so you're a prophet! Well, tell me this: Our ancestors worshiped God at this mountain, but you Jews insist that Jerusalem is the only place for worship, right?"

"Believe me, woman, the time is coming when you Samaritans will worship the Father neither here at this mountain nor there in Jerusalem. You worship guessing in the dark; we Jews worship in the clear light of day. God's way of salvation is made available through the Jews. But the time is coming--it has, In fact, come--when what you're called will

not matter and where you go to worship will not matter. It's who you are and the way you live that count before God. Your worship must engage your spirit in the pursuit of truth. That's the kind of people the Father is out looking for: those who are simply and honestly themselves before him in their worship. God is sheer being itself-- Spirit. Those who worship him must do so out of their very being, their spirits, their true selves, in adoration."

King James says verses 23-24 this way:

But the hour cometh, and now is, when the true worshipers shall worship the Father in spirit and in truth: for the Father seeketh such to worship him. God is a Spirit: and they that worship him must worship him in spirit and in truth.

God is searching among every nation, every kindred, and every tongue, for a people that will worship him in this very way. By his expectations, and no other.

And so, to attempt to worship God in any way, other than with your complete being in full surrender...out of the very reservoirs of your spirit, and with your true selves-in total adoration, is simply not to worship God, at all. ■

Chapter 4
Preparing Him A Place

But I have built an house of habitation for thee, and a place for thy dwelling for ever. (2Chr 6:2)

In the book of Genesis, we find the chronology of the creation of the heavens and the earth.

From day one through day six, God creates the day and night, heaven and earth, dry land and seas, grass, herb yielding seed, fruit tree yielding fruit, sun, moon, stars, living creatures in the seas, fowl in the air, and living creatures on the land (Gen 1:3-26).

Now, God is ready to complete his finest project yet….MAN!

Genesis 1:26-28 records God as saying:

> *…Let us make man in our image, after our likeness: and let them have dominion over the fish of the sea, and over the fowl of the air, and over the cattle, and over all the earth, and over every creeping thing that creepeth upon the earth. So God created man in his own image, in the image of God created he him; male and female created he them. And God blessed them, and God said unto them, Be fruitful, and multiply, and replenish the earth, and subdue it: and have dominion over the fish of the sea, and over the fowl of the air, and over every living thing that moveth upon the earth.*

The word *make* is the Hebrew word *asah* (pron. aw-saw'), and it means to fashion (construct, build, form, shape) accomplish, bestow, appoint, advance, bring forth, and to finish. However, the word *created* is the Hebrew word *bara* (pron. baw-raw'), and means to select, cut down, and to dispatch.

In other words, God fashioned (constructed, built, formed, shaped) you, and bestowed upon you the ability to reflect his nature, and then he cut you down (like a prized tree!), and dispatched you...to accomplish his purpose.

Genesis 2:8 says that "…the LORD God planted a garden eastward in Eden; and there he put the man whom he had formed. The Hebrew word *Eden* (pron. ay'-den) means *garden of pleasure*, or *garden of delight*.

Verse 9 continues on to say that "...out of the ground made the LORD God to grow every tree that is pleasant to the sight, and good for food; the tree of life also in the midst of the garden, and the tree of knowledge of good and evil." God made everything look good and taste good!

Continuing with verses 15-17, the scripture states that "...the Lord God took the man and put him in the Garden of Eden (pleasure, delight) to dress it and to keep it. The Amplified Bible says "...to tend and guard and keep it." The Message Bible says, "...to work the ground and keep it in order."

I wanted a better understanding of the words to *dress* and to *keep*, so I looked deeper. The word *dress* comes from the Hebrew word *abad* (pron. aw-bad'), and it means to **keep,** till, execute, bring to pass, and to serve (or minister). But I noticed two other definitions that I found very interesting. The first was to compel (or induce). And the second was to worship. (Don't worry. I'm coming back to this, in just a moment!)

The word *keep* comes from the Hebrew word *shamar* (pron. shaw-mar'), and it means to guard (mind or **keep**), attend to, preserve, maintain, honor, protect, observe, and wait for.

So, God didn't place man just anywhere. He placed him in an environment that was conducive (favorable, agreeable, beneficial, profitable) to his needs; a place that was pleasant; a place that was serene; a place that was both beautiful and delightful. God placed him in the garden of delight, where his "presence" came "...walking in the garden in the cool of the day"; a place where the God of the universe visited (or touched earth); a place where his creation would wait for him, so that they could enjoy sweet uninterrupted fellowship. Adam had free access to the presence of his creator and friend...God!

God placed him in a garden of pleasure, where he would be compelled to worship, showing excessive love and admiration. He placed him in the garden of his presence, where Adam was to honor, guard, protect, and preserve this "presence". In other words, God told Adam to... "Keep what we have. Don't let anything come between us!" Look at the definition (in bold letters) of *dress* and *keep*. When God does or says a thing twice, he is establishing a principle or a governing law. (See Gen 41:32)

God gave Adam free course in the garden, with one exception (Gen 2:17):
> *You may freely eat of every tree of the garden; But of the tree of the knowledge of good and evil and blessing and calamity you shall not eat, for in the day that you eat of it you shall surely die.*

Adam disobeyed God; he ate of this forbidden tree. In Genesis 3:17, God said to them:

> *Because thou hast hearkened unto the voice of thy wife, and hast eaten of the tree, of which I commanded thee, saying, Thou shalt not eat of it: cursed is the ground for thy sake; in sorrow shalt thou eat of it all the days of thy life; Thorns also and thistles shall it bring forth to thee; and thou shalt eat the herb of the field; In the sweat of thy face shalt thou eat bread, till thou return unto the ground; for out of it wast thou taken: for dust thou art, and unto dust shalt thou return. And Adam called his wife's name Eve; because she was the mother of all living. Unto Adam also and to his wife did the LORD God make coats of skins, and clothed them. And the LORD God said, Behold, the man is become as one of us, to know good and evil: and now, lest he put forth his hand, and take also of the tree of life, and eat, and live for ever: Therefore the LORD God sent him forth from the garden of Eden, to till the ground from whence he was taken. So he drove out the man; and he placed at the east of the garden of Eden Cherubims, and a flaming sword which turned every way, to keep the way of the tree of life.*

The Hebrew word for *drove out* is *garash* (pron. gaw-rash'), and means to drive out or away from your possession; to banish. So, because of man's sin, he was driven away and banished from his greatest possession...God's presence. He now had to live separated from the presence of the Lord. He had to live outside of his ideal environment.

Now, because he had not honored, guarded or protected the garden, Adam, the man that God had created, had given up the privilege of this free, uninhibited access to the presence of God. Therefore God had to guard the way back into his presence. He did this by placing Cherubim and a flaming sword at the entrance of the garden.

From that time, until now, man has been attempting to get back into God's presence, by offering sacrifices for the atonement of their sins. In these early attempts, he built outside altars, where he either invoked God's presence **to** come, or built an altar in memorial in the place where God **had** come.

God set up the initial institution of the Animal Sacrifice, for Genesis 3:21 says, "Unto Adam also and to his wife did the LORD God make coats of skins, and clothed them." (It is obvious that if he obtained coats of animal skin, then an animal had to be sacrificed!) He gave Adam instructions as to what was now the only acceptable form of worship. Now that Adam was a sinner, his sins had to be atoned in this manner. This was to imply worship by faith.

Let's look at a few of these Patriarchs, and some of the altars that they built in preparation for the presence of the Lord.

- **Cain & Abel (Gen 4:3-7)**
  And in process of time it came to pass, that Cain brought of the fruit of the ground an offering unto the LORD. And Abel, he also brought of the firstlings of his flock and of the fat thereof. And the LORD had respect unto Abel and to his offering: But unto Cain and to his offering he had not respect. And Cain was very wroth, and his countenance fell. And the LORD said unto Cain, Why art thou wroth? and why is thy countenance fallen? If thou doest well, shalt thou not be accepted?

Cain and Abel's purpose was to get back into God's presence again...invoking his favor. The difference in their offering was this: Cain brought forth his offering as a simple acknowledgement that God was God. The passage doesn't say anything about it even being the first-fruit of his offering, or the best of his offering. It was just an offering. (It had all the appearance of a proud and unbelieving heart.)

However, Abel brought forth his flock's firstling as a sacrifice for atonement; as an act of worship for a sinner in need of a savior. He gave God the first and the best of his offering, in humbleness, sincerity, and complete obedience (agreement, compliance, submission, subservience, respect). Therefore, God had respect to his offering...and his "presence" came!

- **Noah (Gen 8:20-22)**
  And Noah builded an altar unto the LORD; and took of every clean beast, and of every clean fowl, and offered burnt offerings on the altar. And the LORD smelled a sweet savour; and the LORD said in his heart, I will not again curse the ground any more for man's sake; for the imagination of man's heart is evil from his youth; neither will I again smite any more every thing living, as I have done. While the earth remaineth, seedtime and harvest, and cold and heat, and summer and winter, and day and night shall not cease.

Noah's first act, upon exiting the ark, was to build an altar in thanksgiving to the Creator God that had spared his and his family's lives. God smelled Noah's offering and it was a sweet smell in his nostrils, therefore he blessed him. When God receives our praises, he always bestows a blessing. He makes a promise that he will never again curse the ground (for man's sake), and that he would never destroy every living thing again; this was all because Noah prepared him a place!

- **Abram/Abraham (Gen 12:7-8)**
  And the LORD appeared unto Abram, and said, Unto thy seed will I give this land: and there builded he an altar unto the LORD, who appeared unto him. And he removed from thence unto a mountain on the east of Bethel, and pitched his tent, having Bethel on the west, and Hai on the east: and there he builded an altar unto the LORD, and called upon the name of the LORD.

The first altar was built as a memorial, for the place where God had visited Abram. The second altar, was the place that Abram built, in order to call upon the name of the Lord, to invoke his presence.

Let's look at another passage regarding Abram. He is now in covenant with God, and so his name has been changed to Abraham. It is Genesis 22:1-8:

> And it came to pass after these things, that God did tempt Abraham, and said unto him, Abraham: and he said, Behold, here I am. And he said, Take now thy son, thine only son Isaac, whom thou lovest, and get thee into the land of Moriah; and offer him there for a burnt offering upon one of the mountains which I will tell thee of. And Abraham rose up early in the morning, and saddled his ass, and took two of his young men with him, and Isaac his son, and clave the wood for the burnt offering, and rose up, and went unto the place of which God had told him. Then on the third day Abraham lifted up his eyes, and saw the place afar off. And Abraham said unto his young men, Abide ye here with the ass; and *I and the lad will go yonder and worship*, and come again to you. And Abraham took the wood of the burnt offering, and laid it upon Isaac his son; and he took the fire in his hand, and a knife; and they went both of them together. And Isaac spake unto Abraham his father, and said, My father: and he said, Here am I, my son. And he said, Behold the fire and the wood: but where is the lamb for a burnt offering? And Abraham said, My son, *God will provide himself a lamb* for a burnt offering: so they went both of them together. (Italics mine)

The English translation says, "...God did *tempt* Abraham". The word *tempt* in the Hebrew is *nasah* (pron. naw-saw'), and actually translates to examine (observe or inspect), or to prove.

Abraham knew that he was to sacrifice his only son, but he didn't call it "sacrifice", he called it "worship"! He understood that they were synonymous!

Abraham was in covenant with the Elohiym (the supreme God- exceeding all else), and he knew that one of the covenant rules was that his covenant partner had to "have his back". By faith, he knew that God would meet him there, for he said, "God will provide *himself* a lamb." His covenant partner would show up. His "presence" would be there! (italics mine)

- **Moses (Exo 15:1-2)**
  Then sang Moses and the children of Israel this song unto the LORD, and spake, saying, I will sing unto the LORD, for he hath triumphed gloriously: the horse and his rider hath he thrown into the sea. The LORD is my strength and song, and he is become my salvation: he is my God, and I will prepare him an habitation; my father's God, and I will exalt him.

When God brought Moses and the children of Israel out of Egypt with such a great deliverance, and drowned Pharaoh and his army in the red sea, the first thing that Moses and the Israelites did was to sing a song of celebration; one of exaltation, thanksgiving and praise. After all, Jehovah God (the Lord most vehement, eternal, and self existent) had made a promise to deliver them, and he had kept that promise! Their sole desire was to erect a tabernacle to continually commemorate the faithfulness of this promise-keeping God. And they would build it according to his specifications.

Exo 25:20-22
And the cherubims shall stretch forth their wings on high, covering the mercy seat with their wings, and their faces shall look one to another; toward the mercy seat shall the faces of the cherubims be. And thou shalt put the mercy seat above upon the ark; and in the ark thou shalt put the testimony that I shall give thee. And there I will meet with thee, and I will commune with thee from above the mercy seat, from between the two cherubims which are upon the ark of the testimony, of all things which I will give thee in commandment unto the children of Israel.

Exo 29:40-45
... and shalt do thereto according to the meat offering of the morning, and according to the drink offering thereof, for a sweet savour, an offering made by fire unto the LORD. This shall be a continual burnt offering throughout your generations at the door of the tabernacle of the congregation before the LORD: where I will meet you, to speak there unto thee. And there I will meet with the children of Israel, and the tabernacle shall be sanctified by my glory. And I will sanctify the tabernacle of the congregation, and the altar: I will sanctify also both Aaron and his sons, to minister to me in the priest's office. And I will dwell among the children of Israel, and will be their God.

Lev 9:22-24
And Aaron lifted up his hand toward the people, and blessed them, and came down from offering of the sin offering, and the burnt offering, and peace offerings. And Moses and Aaron went into the tabernacle of the congregation, and came out, and blessed the people: and the glory of the LORD appeared unto all the people. And there came a fire out from before the LORD, and consumed upon the altar the burnt offering and the fat...

God never dwelt with man, until after he had redeemed him (Exodus 34:20). Even afterwards, he still could not dwell with him until he had been sanctified, (or made holy). Remember, his presence was the very thing that Adam had lost in the garden. God gave Moses explicit instructions as to how Aaron and his sons, as well as the tabernacle and the altar, were to be sanctified.

After the sanctification process had been completed, Aaron and his sons were to offer sacrifices unto the Lord. The lamb, offered every morning and every evening as a burnt offering, would be a continual "sweet savor" unto the Lord. And as a result of this perpetual "sweet savor", God would meet and commune with them there...above the mercy seat...between the Cherubim. He would dwell (tabernacle) among them, and be their Elohiym (Supreme God).

- **Nadab & Abihu (Lev 10:1-2)**
  And Nadab and Abihu, the sons of Aaron, took either of them his censer, and put fire therein, and put incense thereon, and offered strange fire before the LORD, which he commanded them not. And there went out fire from the LORD, and devoured them, and they died before the LORD.

Just as Cain had done, Nadab and Abihu offered unto the Lord an offering that did not please him. They proceeded to encroach into the Holy of Holies, presuming to take upon them the responsibility that God had only authorized the High Priest (their father, Aaron) to perform. Their perpetrated act of willful disobedience resulted in death. What God had designed to be a most worshipful act turned into contempt, when they did not adhere to God's explicit directions. A holy act was made unholy. Hebrews 12:14 says, "Follow...holiness, without which no man shall see the Lord."

- **David (Psa 132:3-5)**
  Surely I will not come into the tabernacle of my house, nor go up into my bed; I will not give sleep to mine eyes, or slumber to mine eyelids, Until I find out a place for the LORD, an habitation for the mighty God of Jacob.

1 Chr 15:1
And David…prepared a place for the ark of God, and pitched for it a tent.

As a boy, David had perfected worship. And because of his passionate pursuit of God, God made him both king and priest. David would spend many hours (and at times, all night) sitting in the presence of Jehovah God. There, he would commune and fellowship with him in the temporary tent that he had prepared for the ark; and God would meet him as he offered up both the burnt sacrifices and the sacrifices of praise, from the "fruit" of his lips.

1 Chr 22:5
And David said, Solomon my son is young and tender, and the house that is to be builded for the LORD must be exceeding magnifical, of fame and of glory throughout all countries: I will therefore now make preparation for it. So David prepared abundantly before his death.

David desired to build God a permanent dwelling place, but God (through the prophet Nathan) said that it would not be built until after David's death. However, his promise to David was that his son Solomon would build it.

So, David gives Solomon instructions on how to build the place of the Lord's permanent dwelling. It is not to be a fortuitous undertaking. He must properly plan. Neither is the building to be a mediocre undertaking, but must be exceeding (surpassing) beautiful, exceeding (outdoing) magnificent, and exceeding (beyond) impressive. He must prepare in abundance. No expense is to be spared. He must hire the best stone masons, the best carpenters, the best blacksmiths, the best tailors, the best iron cutters, etc… It is God's house! the best of everything must be used. The fame and glory of it must go out to all countries. It must (especially!) supersede the temple where the pagan goddess Diana is worshiped. This temple is to be built for the God of all gods. It must be built like God's name- Elohiym….Exceeding All Else.

- **Solomon (2 Chr 2:1)**
  And Solomon determined to build an house for the name of the LORD, and an house for his kingdom.

  2 Chr 2:1;4-5
  …I have built an house of habitation for thee, and a place for thy dwelling for ever. Behold, I build an house to the name of the LORD my God, to dedicate it to him, and to burn before him sweet incense, and for the continual shewbread, and for the burnt offerings morning and evening, on the sabbaths, and on the new moons, and on the solemn feasts of the

> *LORD our God. This is an ordinance for ever to Israel. And the house which I build is great: for great is our God above all gods.*

Solomon follows the instructions of his father, obeying God's charge. God now has a permanent dwelling (not excluding the rebuilding of the temple- Ezra 1:5; 3:10-13). There, they will offer sacrifices until Christ (the Lamb) is sacrificed. He, offering up his blood (being received by the Father), obtains eternal redemption; and ascending to him, leaves the Comforter (the Holy Spirit) to dwell within man (Acts 1:8;2:1-4). Ahhh... his final resting place!

- **Paul (Eph 2:20-22)**
  As fellow citizens, we are "...built upon the foundation of the apostles and prophets, Jesus Christ himself being the chief corner stone; In whom all the building fitly framed together groweth unto an holy temple in the Lord: In whom ye also are builded together for an habitation of God through the Spirit.

In the Message Bible, the same passage reads:

> *He used the apostles and prophets for the foundation. Now he's using you, fitting you in brick by brick, stone by stone, with Christ Jesus as the cornerstone that holds all the parts together. We see it taking shape day after day--a holy temple built by God, all of us built into it, a temple in which God is quite at home.*

When a builder prepares to build on a piece of land, he must first excavate that land. He has to clear it of all of the large rocks, boulders, trees, tree stumps, bushes, and other debris. Then he must level the land, so that the foundation will be even. Then he pours the foundation. If the foundation is stable (steady, firm, sure), then the building will be able to withstand any strong winds, storms, or floods that may come against it.

Now the Holy Spirit lives in earthen vessels. The apostle's job is to lay a proper foundation, so that you will learn how to properly prepare a place for His "dwelling". He must give you proper instruction, so that you will learn how to do maintenance work in order to help protect, and keep your temple clean. This is so your temple will be able to withstand any strong winds, storms, or floods that may come against it.

Just as the temple at Jerusalem was exceeding beautiful, exceeding magnificent, and exceeding in its impressiveness, this earthen temple exceeds all man-made temples, for it was sculpted by Elohiym, himself. This is the temple where the God of the universe has chosen to make his abode!

The Apostle Paul asks the Corinthians, "Know ye not that ye are the temple of God, and that the Spirit of God dwelleth in you?" (1 Cor 3:16) And again in 1 Corinthians 6:19, he poses this question, "What? know ye not that your body is the temple of the Holy Ghost which is in you, which ye have of God, and ye are not your own?"

You may ask, "All this is well and good, but how do we prepare him a place?"

I'm glad that you've asked.

In order to prepare Him a place to make his abode, I believe that there are at least 7 things that we must do. Below, I list them, with songs and scriptures, to help support my belief.

(1) We prepare him a place by inviting him to come in.

There's a favorite Christmas Carol of the church, and its 1st verse goes like this:

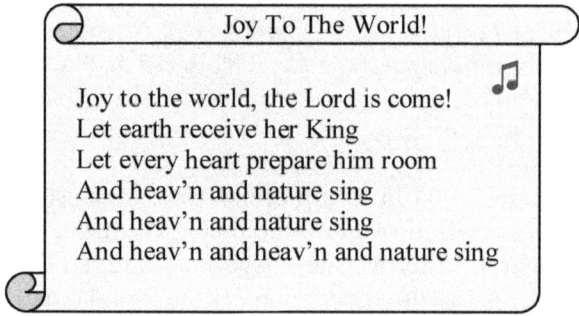

Jesus says in Revelations 3:20, "Behold, I stand at the door, and knock: if any man hear my voice, and open the door, I will come in to him, and will sup with him, and he with me."

Paul's prayer for the Ephesian church was "That Christ may dwell in your hearts by faith." (Eph 3:17)

In the Message Bible, that same passage reads, "That Christ will live in you as you open the door and invite him in."

Paul, speaking to the Corinthian church (2 Cor 6:16b), exclaims, "...for ye are the temple of the living God; as God hath said, I will dwell in them, and walk in them; and I will be their God, and they shall be my people."

(2) We prepare him a place by having a broken spirit.

There is another song, that I wrote. The verse goes like this:

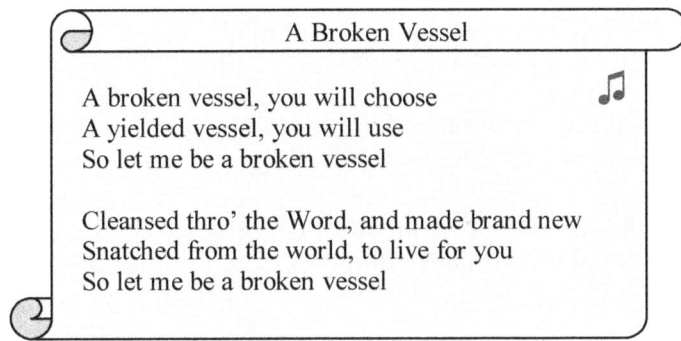

A Broken Vessel

A broken vessel, you will choose
A yielded vessel, you will use
So let me be a broken vessel

Cleansed thro' the Word, and made brand new
Snatched from the world, to live for you
So let me be a broken vessel

David avows in Psalms 51:17, "The sacrifices of God are a broken spirit: a broken and a contrite heart, O God, thou wilt not despise."

In Psalms 34:18, he states, "The LORD is nigh unto them that are of a broken heart; and saveth such as be of a contrite spirit."

In Isaiah 57:15, the prophet declares, "For thus saith the high and lofty One that inhabiteth eternity, whose name is Holy; I dwell in the high and holy place, with him also that is of a contrite and humble spirit, to revive the spirit of the humble, and to revive the heart of the contrite ones."

And God, speaking in verse 66:2 says, "…but to this man will I look, even to him that is poor and of a contrite spirit, and trembleth at my word."

(3) We prepare him a place by keeping our temple clean.

In preparation before going to minister in Germany, a few years ago, the Spirit of the Lord gave me this song.

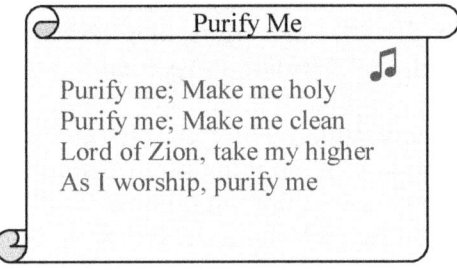

Purify Me

Purify me; Make me holy
Purify me; Make me clean
Lord of Zion, take my higher
As I worship, purify me

Paul declares to the church at Corinth (1 Cor 3:17), "If any man defile the temple of God, him shall God destroy; for the temple of God is holy, which temple ye are." He also bids them, "Flee fornication. Every sin that a man doeth is without the body; but he that committeth fornication sinneth against his own body. What? know ye not that your body is the temple of the Holy Ghost which is in you, which ye have of God, and ye are not your own?"

He questions them, in 2 Corinthians 6:16, asking, "And what agreement hath the temple of God with idols? for ye are the temple of the living God."

Jesus said to the scribes and Pharisees in Jerusalem (Mat 15:18), "...those things which proceed out of the mouth come forth from the heart; and they defile the man."

Lastly, Paul, entreats the church at Rome (Rom 12:1), saying, "I beseech you therefore, brethren, by the mercies of God, that ye present your bodies a living sacrifice, holy, acceptable unto God, which is your reasonable service."

(4) We prepare him a place by keeping our hearts clean.

This is a song that I wrote, years ago. (Alright, so I've got another song! After all, I am a Psalmist.):

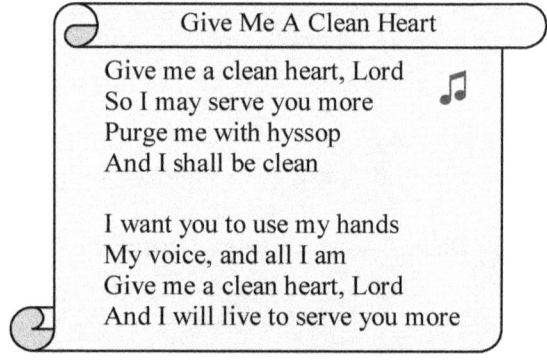

Give Me A Clean Heart

Give me a clean heart, Lord
So I may serve you more
Purge me with hyssop
And I shall be clean

I want you to use my hands
My voice, and all I am
Give me a clean heart, Lord
And I will live to serve you more

Peter, writing to the exiles scattered throughout Pontus, Galatia, Cappadocia, Asia, and Bithynia (1 Pet 2:1 Message Bible) implores them, asserting, "So clean house! Make a clean sweep of malice and pretense, envy and hurtful talk."

Job's "friend" (Zophar), encouraging Job to repent (Job 11:13-15), says, "If thou prepare thine heart, and stretch out thine hands toward him; If iniquity be in thine hand, put it far away, and let not wickedness dwell in thy tabernacles. For then shalt thou lift up thy face without spot; yea, thou shalt be stedfast, and shalt not fear."

In Psalms 51:7-10, David prays to God, crying out, "Purge me with hyssop, and I shall be clean: wash me, and I shall be whiter than snow. Make me to hear joy and gladness; that the bones which thou hast broken may rejoice. Hide thy face from my sins, and blot out all mine iniquities. Create in me a clean heart, O God; and renew a right spirit within me."

And Lastly, in Matthew 5:8, Jesus tenderly teaches, "Blessed are the pure in heart: for they shall see God."

(5) We prepare him a place by keeping our hands clean.

This is another song, that the Lord has given me.

In Psalms 24:4, David declares, "He that hath clean hands, and a pure heart; who hath not lifted up his soul unto vanity, nor sworn deceitfully."

David avows in Psalms 26:6 (MSG), "I scrub my hands with purest soap, then join hands with the others in the great circle, dancing around your altar, GOD…"

(6) We prepare him a place by keeping our minds renewed.

Yes! Another song.

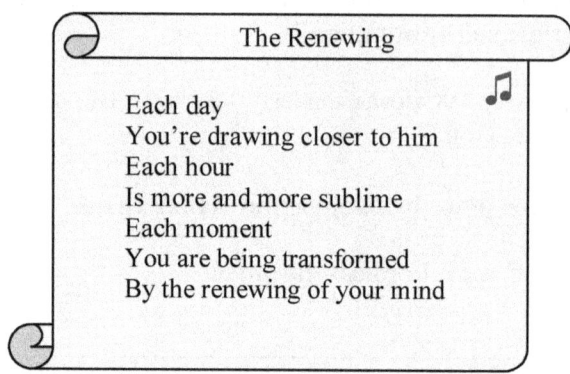

Paul encourages the church at Ephesus to "...be renewed in the spirit of your mind..." (Eph 4:23)

He urges the church at Rome to "...be not conformed to this world: but be ye transformed by the renewing of your mind, that ye may prove what is that good, and acceptable, and perfect, will of God." (Rom 12:2)

Also teaching them, he asserts, "Focusing on the self is the opposite of focusing on God. Anyone completely absorbed in self ignores God, ends up thinking more about self than God. That person ignores who God is and And God isn't pleased at being ignored. But if God himself has taken up residence in your life, you can hardly be thinking more of yourself than of him. But for you who welcome him, in whom he dwells--even though you still experience all the limitations of sin--you yourself experience life on God's terms." (Rom 8:7-10 Message Bible)

Paul, writing to the church at Philippi, commands, "Let this mind be in you, which was also in Christ Jesus..." (Phi 2:5)

And Paul, writing to Titus (his spiritual son), teaches, "Unto the pure all things are pure: but unto them that are defiled and unbelieving is nothing pure; but even their mind and conscience is defiled." (Tit 1:15)

(7) We prepare him a place by having no other gods before him.

This is an old Hymn that I wrote, some years ago.

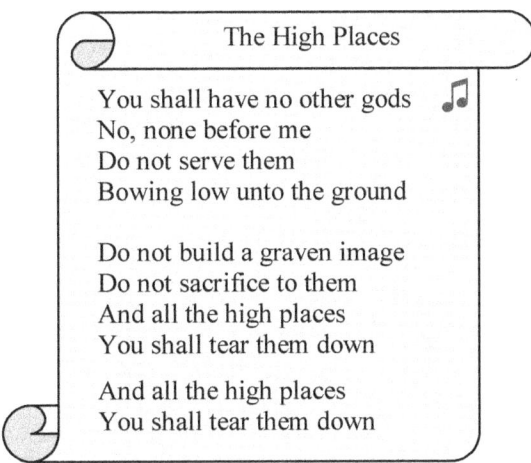

In Exodus 20:3-5, God gives the Children of Israel the 10 commandments or governing laws, that he wrote on tablets for Moses to implement. Let's look at this passage:

Thou shalt have no other gods before me. Thou shalt not make unto thee any graven image, or any likeness of any thing that is in heaven above, or that is in the earth beneath, or that is in the water under the earth: Thou shalt not bow down thyself to them, nor serve them.

In Exodus 34:11-17, God is more specific, as he commands the children of Israel to observe his laws:

Observe thou that which I command thee this day: behold, I drive out before thee the Amorite, and the Canaanite, and the Hittite, and the Perizzite, and the Hivite, and the Jebusite. Take heed to thyself, lest thou make a covenant with the inhabitants of the land whither thou goest, lest it be for a snare in the midst of thee: But ye shall destroy their altars, break their images, and cut down their groves: For thou shalt worship no other god: for the LORD, whose name is Jealous, is a jealous God: Lest thou make a covenant with the inhabitants of the land, and they go a whoring after their gods, and do sacrifice unto their gods, and one call thee, and thou eat of his sacrifice; And thou take of their daughters unto thy sons, and their daughters go a whoring after their gods, and make thy sons go a whoring after their gods. Thou shalt make thee no molten gods.

Leviticus 19:4, he again warns them, commanding, "Turn ye not unto idols, nor make to yourselves molten gods: I am the LORD your God."

Once again, he warns his people (Deu 20:17-18):

> *But thou shalt utterly destroy them; namely, the Hittites, and the Amorites, the Canaanites, and the Perizzites, the Hivites, and the Jebusites; as the LORD thy God hath commanded thee: as the LORD thy God hath commanded thee: That they teach you not to do after all their abominations, which they have done unto their gods; so should ye sin against the LORD your God.*

You would think that with such a great deliverance as the children of Israel saw at the Red Sea, that they would be sold out to the Lord "lot, stock, and barrel". Not!

The children of Israel did not obey the voice of the Lord, time and time again. They went constantly "whoring" after other gods, bowing down to them, and worshiping them. All the other nations were jealous of their god, but they just couldn't see it! They were in covenant with the Elohiym (the God that exceeds all other gods), and Jehovah (the Alpha & Omega); and yet, they wanted to be like all the other nations, as they would later, emphatically declare (1Samuel 8:5b), "Now make us a king to judge us like all the nations"!

In Isaiah 42:8, God speaks through Isaiah proclaiming, "I am the LORD: that is my name: and my glory will I not give to another, neither my praise to graven images."

God says what he means, and means what he says, as Solomon would so tragically discover.

Solomon, the son of King David, had now become king after David's death. In Gibeon, as Solomon was asleep, God visited him in a dream. God asked Solomon what he wanted from him. Solomon asked for wisdom. God told him that because he hadn't asked for riches or for honor, it would be given him, anyway. He also told him that there would be no king before him or after him with such wisdom, riches and honor. All God asked, was that Solomon walk in his ways, and keep his statutes and commandments. But Solomon couldn't.

Let's follow the story in 1 Kings (verses 1-11):

> *But king Solomon loved many strange women, together with the daughter of Pharaoh, women of the Moabites, Ammonites, Edomites, Zidonians, and Hittites; Of the nations concerning which the LORD said unto*

the children of Israel, Ye shall not go in to them, neither shall they come in unto you: for surely they will turn away your heart after their gods: Solomon clave unto these in love. And he had seven hundred wives, princesses, and three hundred concubines: and his wives turned away his heart. For it came to pass, when Solomon was old, that his wives turned away his heart after other gods: and his heart was not perfect with the LORD his God, as was the heart of David his father. For Solomon went after Ashtoreth the goddess of the Zidonians, and after Milcom the abomination of the Ammonites. And Solomon did evil in the sight of the LORD, and went not fully after the LORD, as did David his father. Then did Solomon build an high place for Chemosh, the abomination of Moab, in the hill that is before Jerusalem, and for Molech, the abomination of the children of Ammon. And likewise did he for all his strange wives, which burnt incense and sacrificed unto their gods. And the LORD was angry with Solomon, because his heart was turned from the LORD God of Israel, which had appeared unto him twice, And had commanded him concerning this thing, that he should not go after other gods: but he kept not that which the LORD commanded. Wherefore the LORD said unto Solomon, Forasmuch as this is done of thee, and thou hast not kept my covenant and my statutes, which I have commanded thee, I will surely rend the kingdom from thee, and will give it to thy servant.

Notice that this scripture passage doesn't say that Solomon totally abandoned God. It says that he was not "perfect", in that he didn't follow "...*fully* after the Lord" (Italics mine). He had allowed his heart to be turned.

The word *turned*, in 1 Kings 11:4, is the Hebrew word *natah* (pron. naw-taw'), and means to overthrow, cause to decline, weaken, carry aside, fail, regress, or bow down.

So, Solomon had caused his heart to decline from following God perfectly. He had bowed his heart to other gods. This was in total defiance to God's Law which commanded: "Thou shalt not bow down thyself to them, nor serve them."

Contrary to public opinion, God does give his people warnings. He had given Solomon at least 3 warnings: One, in the Law itself, and twice he had appeared personally to Solomon. Solomon knew the Law, and he knew what would happen if he disobeyed God's Law; and yet, he proceeded to do so with his eyes wide open. He had yielded to the same sin that had brought Adam down: the lust of the flesh, the lust of the eyes, and the pride of life.

In Psalms 81:9-14, David describes what would happen to a people who would not hearken unto God's voice:

There shall no strange god be in thee; neither shalt thou worship any strange god. I am the LORD thy God, which brought thee out of the land of Egypt: open thy mouth wide, and I will fill it. But my people would not hearken to my voice; and Israel would none of me. So I gave them up unto their own hearts' lust: and they walked in their own counsels. Oh that my people had hearkened unto me, and Israel had walked in my ways! I should soon have subdued their enemies, and turned my hand against their adversaries.

This is such a tragic end for someone whom God had blessed above all others.

This, by no means, exhausts everything that you may have to do in order to prepare him room; Those things that I had to give up, may not be the things that he's asking you to give up. But whatever the cost, by all means, give it up... preparing him a place of permanent residence.

Don't end up like Solomon. Allow God to live in you, breathe in you, walk in you, and make changes in you. Allow him show you the high places that you've erected to the lust of your flesh, the lust of your eyes, and the pride of life. Obey his voice, as he gingerly pleads with you to tear down those high places, completely, and follow fully after him. Allow him to sit on the throne of your heart, ruling both your heart and mind. Allow him to be Jehovah Elohiym- exceeding all else- in your life. ∎

Chapter 5
The Praise of Judah

And she conceived again, and bare a son: and she said, Now will I praise the LORD: therefore she called his name Judah... (Gen. 29:35)

Jacob, obeying his father Isaac had not taken a wife of the people of Canaan, but had gone to his mother's people in Padan-Aram...to the house of Bethual. There, her brother Laban lived with his two daughters, Leah and Rachel. Leah was tender-eyed (or weak eyed, inferring that she was cross-eyed), but Rachel was beautiful, and well favored.

Jacob fell in love with the younger of the two...Rachel, and agreed to pay Laban the price of 7 years labor for her. Because of his deep love for her, those years passed quickly. For him, it seemed as though only days had past. However, he fell to inquire as to their customs; one of their customs was that the youngest should not marry before the eldest.

So, on his wedding night, after an elaborate wedding feast (and much wine!), Jacob entered the wedding chamber with his bride, Rachel, only to find out in the morning, that it wasn't Rachel, at all, but Leah! (Can you imagine the shock on his face?!?)

After the shock wears off, and after an (understandably) upset Jacob discusses the issue with his father-in-law, they come to an agreement. Jacob agrees to work another 7 years for Rachel. She would be given to him in marriage, once he has fulfilled his week with Leah.

Despite Leah's great love for Jacob, Jacob could not return it. She was not only unloved by her husband, but the Genesis 29:31 even goes further to say that God took notice that Leah was hated by her husband. And to add "salt to injury", she had to share him with her younger sister...his beloved Rachel. And because, he did not love Leah, God shut Rachel's womb, but blessed Leah's.

The number four (4) in Prophecy means the changing of seasons, the changing of directions, intervention, and also means lamentation (or the inability to celebrate or rejoice).

Leah had lamented (expressed great grief or sorrow) for not being loved, and God had blessed her womb, by given her three sons: Reuben, Simeon, and Levi...but it wasn't enough!

Reuben means *behold, God has given me a son*. With Reuben, she believed that her husband would love her, but she was still not satisfied. *Satisfied* means to be content, fulfilled, gratified, placated (or soothed). Leah did not feel soothed. So, God gave her *Simeon*, which means *God has heard me*. She believed that God had heard the fact that Jacob had hated her. But still not satisfied, she had another son. This time she named him *Levi*, which means *attached*. This third son, she believed, would surely cause Jacob to be joined to her, because she had born him three sons. But she was still not satisfied.

So, still lamenting, Genesis 29:35 declares:

> *And she conceived again, and bare a son: and she said, Now will I praise the LORD: therefore she called his name Judah; and left bearing.*

Judah (pron. yeh-hoo-daw'), as the above scripture declares, means *praise,* or actually *celebrated*. It is based on the Hebrew word *yadah* (pron. yaw-daw'), which means to use or hold out the hand, inferring to praise, revere, or worship with extended hands. Another definition is to cast, shoot, throw, or aim towards. It also means to make confession, to give praise or thanks.

Let's look at a few scriptures using this word *Judah*.

The first, is Genesis 49:8-12 (MSG). Before Jacob's exit off of life's stage, he calls his sons in; and calling them to his bedside, one by one, he prophesies over them. Hear what he says about Judah:

> *You, Judah, your brothers will praise you: Your fingers on your enemies' throat, while your brothers honor you. You're a lion's cub, Judah, home fresh from the kill, my son. Look at him, crouched like a lion, The scepter shall not leave Judah; he'll keep a firm grip on the command staff Until the ultimate ruler comes and the nations obey him. He'll tie up his donkey to the grapevine, his purebred prize to a sturdy branch. He will wash his shirt in wine and his cloak in the blood of grapes, His eyes will be darker than wine, his teeth whiter than milk.*

Jacob is saying, that we don't really have to fight the enemy. All we have to do, is lift up praise to the Lord. And as we do, our praise will become as fingers, in the shape of a choke hold, around the enemy's neck. Jacob understood the same thing that David would be quoted later, saying: "The battle is the Lord's."

Webster defines the word *scepter*, as the rod, wand, insignia, crest, or staff of a monarch's authority. Judah has the authority to come before God's presence. Psalms 76:1-2 declares, "In Judah is God known: his name is great in Israel. In Salem also is his tabernacle, and his dwelling place in Zion."

Now, substituting the word *praise* for the word Judah, the same scripture would read, "In *praise* is God known: His name is great in Israel. In Salem also is his tabernacle, and his dwelling place in Zion."

When God gave Moses the plan for the Tabernacle, he also gave him orders on how the tribes were to encamp round about it. Here, in Numbers 2:1-3, the Lord speaks, saying:

> *Every man of the children of Israel shall pitch by his own standard, with the ensign of their father's house: far off about the tabernacle of the congregation shall they pitch. And on the east side toward the rising of the sun shall they of the standard of the camp of Judah pitch throughout their armies: and Nahshon the son of Amminadab shall be captain of the children of Judah.*

Henry's Commentary makes this note regarding the Lord's comment of this tribe:

> The tribe of Judah was in the first post of honour, encamped towards the rising sun, and in their marches led the van, not only because it was the most numerous tribe, but chiefly because from that tribe Christ was to come, who is the Lion of the tribe of Judah…

Are you enjoying this? I am. Let's continue with a few more scriptures, shall we?

At this point in Israel's history, the great man of God, Moses, has died, and so has the next appointed leader, Joshua. But the Canaanites continue to war against them. In Judges 1:1-2, 4 & 19, God, again, reveals Judah's destiny:

> *Now after the death of Joshua it came to pass, that the children of Israel asked the LORD, saying, Who shall go up for us against the Canaanites first, to fight against them? And the LORD said, Judah shall go up: behold, I have delivered the land into his hand.*

> *And Judah went up; and the LORD delivered the Canaanites and the Perizzites into their hand…*

> *And the LORD was with Judah; and he drave out the inhabitants of the mountain…*

And again when Israel went up against the tribe of Benjamin (Jud 20:18) for acts of lewdness and the murder of a Levite's concubine:

> *And the children of Israel arose, and went up to the house of God, and*

asked counsel of God, and said, Which of us shall go up first to the battle against the children of Benjamin? And the LORD said, Judah shall go up first.

You see, in a battle, you place the strongest warriors with weapons in the front.

This is your first line of defense against any enemy, as well as your first line of offense against your enemy. However, God told them to let Judah go up first. Why? Because praise is a spiritual weapon, and is much stronger, than any earthly weapon. God was setting precedence: If we praise him first, then the battle belongs to him! He will fight for us!

When fighting Goliath (1 Samuel 17:45), David, the great praiser of Israel, said to him:

Thou comest to me with a sword, and with a spear, and with a shield: but I come to thee in the name of the LORD of hosts, the God of the armies of Israel, whom thou hast defied.

In Psalms 114:1-2, David avers, "Judah was his sanctuary, and Israel his dominion." In other words, in Israel, God rules and governs. Over them, he has power and authority. But, Judah is his sacred place; his holy place. He lives in the midst of Judah. He inhabits Judah.

Let me give you this little example:

Queen Elizabeth rules over all of England. It is the place of her power and authority. It is her domain, where she rules and governs.

However, she dwells in London. That is her sacred place; her sanctuary. That is the place where she lives.

One last scripture affirms this. It is Psalms 78:67-68 (AMP):

Moreover, He rejected the tent of Joseph and chose not the tribe of Ephraim [*in which the tabernacle had been accustomed to stand*]. But He chose the tribe of Judah [*as Israel's leader*], Mount Zion, which He loved [*to replace Shiloh as His capital*].

God had chosen the tribe of Judah as the seat of the Ark of his presence.

Now, let's look at a few scriptures using *yadah*...the Hebrew word for praise, from which Judah was derived.

The first is found in Nehemiah 12:46. Nehemiah notes, "For in the days of David and Asaph of old there were chief of the singers, and songs of praise and *thanksgiving* unto God." Now, for this word, *thanksgiving*, yadah is used.

I know that we've already looked at Psalms 100:4, but let's peruse it a little further:

> Enter into his gates with thanksgiving (todah), and into his courts with praise (tehillah): be *thankful* (yadah) unto him, and bless his name.

What David is actually saying here is that we must enter into the first level of thanksgiving as a willing sacrifice (todah), and then into his courts with a praise song resounding in our spirit (tehillah). Then, we must yadah (lift up our hands, aiming all energy and efforts toward the mark) unto him (God), and bless (barak) his name.

As I stated earlier, *yadah* also means to make confession (admission or acknowledgement of guilt or of goodness shown), as in 2 Chronicles 30, verse 22 (Parentheses mine):

> And Hezekiah spoke comfortably unto all the Levites that taught the good knowledge of the LORD: and they did eat throughout the feast seven days, offering peace offerings, and *making confession* (yadah) to the LORD God of their fathers.

Daniel pens, in chapter 9, verse 3, "And I set my face unto the Lord God, to seek by prayer and supplications, with fasting, and sackcloth, and ashes:" And, in verse 4 he asserts, "And I prayed unto the LORD my God, and *made my confession* (yadah), and said..."

Let's take a look at a few more scriptures that denote yadah.

In 2 Samuel 22:50, and also in Psalms 18:49, David declares (yadah being substituted):

> Therefore I will give yadah (thanks by lifting up my hands, and aiming my praise) unto thee, O LORD, among the heathen, and I will sing praises unto thy name. (parentheses mine).

1 Chronicles 16:8, David states, "Give *thanks* (yadah) unto the LORD, call upon his name, make known his deeds among the people." Again, in 1 Chronicles 16:34, Psalms 107:1, 118:29, and 136:1, David proclaims, "O give *thanks* (yadah) unto the LORD; for he is good; for his mercy endureth forever."

Also, in 1 Chronicles 16:41, David makes note that "...with them Heman and

Jeduthun, and the rest that were chosen, who were expressed by name…" gave "*thanks* (yadah) to the LORD, because his mercy endureth forever…"

So here, we see people assigned to actually lift up their hands, and "aim" their praises to the Lord.

Here in Psalms 119:61, David boldly confesses, "The bands of the wicked have robbed me: but I have not forgotten thy law." And in verse 62, he declares, "At midnight I will rise to give *thanks* (yadah) to thee because of thy righteous judgments." David is declaring that no care of grief should be so bad as to rob the word of God from our mouths, and keep us from making haste to glorify God. Even at the "midnights" in our lives, we can arise without effort and enjoy giving thanks and praise to our God.

We're almost finished. But, let's look at Ezra's account (Ezra 3:11):

> And they sang together by course in praising and giving *thanks* (yadah) unto the LORD; because he is good, for his mercy endureth forever toward Israel. And all the people shouted with a great shout, when they praised the LORD, because the foundation of the house of the LORD was laid.

So, as their minds were becoming more and more submissive, and as they made open confession before the Lord, they actually went from a level of effort to a level of enjoyment. They actually began to enjoy singing praises unto the Lord! And the more they sang and shouted, the more they enjoyed giving thanks. Why? Because the more they offered affirmations, the more they reaffirmed to themselves this fact …that…the Lord **is** good, and his mercy **does** endure forever!

In 1Chronicles 28:4, David declares, "He hath chosen Judah to be the ruler (or governor)," and in Psalms 108:8, God, speaking through David asserts, "Gilead is mine; Manasseh is mine; Ephraim also is the strength of mine head; Judah is my lawgiver (appointee, decreer, governor)…"

David is declaring that your praise will govern your outcome. Let me prove it to you. ('Better hold on to your socks)!

Before Moses dies, he blesses each of the tribes of Israel. In Deuteronomy 33:7, regarding Judah, he says:

> *Hear, LORD, the voice of Judah, and bring him unto his people: let his hands be sufficient for him; and be thou an help to him from his enemies.*

Earlier, we talked about the meaning of numbers in prophecy. Well, the number 4 in Prophecy also means the number of divine intervention.

Yadah, the Hebrew word from which Judah is derived, comes from the Hebrew word *yad*, meaning the "open" hand. One of the definitions of yad is axletree.

An axle is a pin, hinge, or axis. It is crucial in the overall function of a car. Why?

Because, the axle allows your car to make turns. Your car cannot turn a corner without it. You will simple keep straight. Other definitions of axle include the words pivot, or turning point.

What God is trying to reveal through his word is this. (Get ready to have a hallelujah fit!)

If you don't like the situation you're in, all you have to do is offer up thanksgiving (yadah) to God (enjoying it!). Lift up your hands, aiming your praises toward him. Your praises will be on the neck of your enemy, choking the "life" out of him. Your praise will send out a decree (or divine order) regarding your situation. Your praise will a *change of Seasons* in your circumstances! It will cause a *change of directions* in your circumstances! It will cause *divine intervention!* Your praise will act like an *axle*, and turn your situation for the good! It will cause you to be able to *celebrate*, once again!

Well go ahead! Start yadah'ing the Lord, and watch your situation and circumstances turn!

Chapter 6
Praise

But thou art holy, O thou that inhabitest the praises of Israel. (Psa 22:3)

𝒫*raise* is a concept that is much easier to understand than its companion, Worship. Why? It is simple. Praise is something that we do almost every single day. We praise our employees for doing a great job. We praise our children for doing their chores or making good grades. We praise our dogs when they obey our commands. Praise is something that comes natural to most people.

In regards to our "Praise" experience, praise is generally classified as standing, hand lifting, clapping, dancing, leaping, etc…, in celebration **to** God for what he has done (direct or vertical praise). Praise is also something we express to others **about** God (indirect or horizontal praise). It is more "fleshy" (being more physical than worship). Praise is concerned with God's character -as well as- his glorious and wonderful acts toward us, his children. We praise God for what he has done, is doing, and is able to do for us in the future. Praise benefits us, not God. God doesn't need our praise. We, however, need to praise God.

Praise is located in the area called "Time". How do I know this? Have you noticed that you are usually "gun ho" when praise starts, but after a while (in Time!), your flesh starts to feel tired, and you almost give up the "good fight"? You have to make a conscious effort to continue to "praise" Him. But that is exactly what is supposed to happen. Your flesh is supposed to get tired…get tired…and DIE!

Moses, being instructed by God, built the Tabernacle, which consisted of the Outer Court, the Holy Place, and the Most Holy Place (also called The Holiest or The Holy of Holies).

In the Outer Court, the Brazen Altar was located. This was the place where the choicest of specific animals were sacrificed unto God. As the animal's flesh burned, its smell entered the Father's nostrils. And as it did, he remembered his people Israel, and met their needs.

Using this typology, Praise is an Outer Court experience. In Romans 12:1, Paul entreats the church at Rome, saying, "I beseech you therefore, brethren, by the mercies of God, that ye present your bodies a living sacrifice, holy, acceptable unto God, which is your reasonable service." It is the same principle of the animal sacrifice: Let your flesh die, so that the aroma of your dead flesh will enter the Father's nostrils. And as it enters the Father's nostrils, he will remember you. How? The Father knows your smell. And as he smells you, he remembers the prayers that you've lifted up and placed before him, and he answers them and meets your needs.

In Psalms 100:4, the Psalmist David says that we must "Enter into his gates with *thanksgiving*, and into his courts with praise: be thankful unto him, and bless his name."

I remember the first time I traveled to Montego Bay, Jamaica. I went with a mission-team made up of musicians. On one particular day, we had made plans to go out, door to door with flyers, to promote a worship service that we were going to have that night. It was to be held in the local White House district. Prior to going out, we were "schooled" on local etiquette.

We learned that most of the locals have fenced in "gardens" (or yards). When you approach someone's garden, you never proceed to open the gate and walk on in. You stand at the gate and yell, "Yoo-hoo!" This is to alert them that you are trying to get their attention. You might be looking right at the residence. But unless they respond to you by saying, "Come", you are not welcomed to enter the gate.

However, once you've entered the gate, you must wait in the courtyard, until they bid you to come up to their porch. And then, or course, they must open the door, allowing you to enter into their "inner chambers" (or home).

Just like you must first say, "Yoo-hoo", in order to enter into a Jamaican's gate, you must first offer thanksgiving…a willing sacrifice of praise…. This is your "yoo-hoo" that alerts the Father that you are trying to get his attention. This is to let him know that you desire to enter into his "gates". When you've given proper thanksgiving, he will bid you to come into his courts with praise (perpetual or continuous hymns or songs of laudation). If he doesn't respond to you by saying, "Come", you are not welcomed to enter his gates.

Each step of the way, from his gates, to his courts, to the holy place, and into the holiest, is a journey of acceptance.

In Psalms 116:17, David declares, "I will offer to thee the sacrifice of *thanksgiving*, and will call upon the name of the LORD."

The word here, *offer*, is the Hebrew word *zabach* (pron. zaw-bakh'), and means to slaughter or to kill. The word *sacrifice*, is a derivative of zabach, and is *zebach* (pron. zeh'- bakh). It means, of course, the same thing. Let me expound on this.

David is saying that when death is staring us in the face and hell is hard at our heals, and all we can find is trouble and sorrow, and we ask ourselves, "What shall we offer the Lord for all of his generosity toward us?" David sees past the hell on earth, and sees the goodness of heaven, and says, "I know what we shall offer him. Although we're fighting, daily, for our very existence, and although we're fighting hell itself...with death all around us, we will make ourselves offer the Lord praise. We will die to ourselves, killing our flesh, and **this** we will offer to the Lord as a praise offering."

It is, indeed, a sacrifice, but as Paul declares, "It is also our reasonable (fair, level-headed, sensible, sound, just, rational, practical) service." (Parentheses mine)

In Hebrews 13:15, Paul implores the saints to... "offer the sacrifice of praise to God continually, that is, the fruit of our lips giving thanks to his name."

In 2 Corinthian 2:15, Paul says, "For we are unto God a *sweet savor* of Christ..." In the Message Bible, the same scripture states, "Because of Christ, we give off a *sweet scent* rising to God..." (Italics mine)

The word *savor* comes from the Greek word *euodia* (pron. yoo-o-dee'-ah) and means just what it says: sweet smelling, aroma (or good scentedness).

In other words, when we praise God, we give off a pure, delightful, pleasant, pleasing, agreeable, satisfying, gratifying, and enjoyable scent.

One meaning of the word *sweet*, is sugary. But it also means melodious, harmonious, tuneful, or musical. As a musician, that excites me; to know that my smell...my incense...my very aroma rises as a harmonious melody into his nostrils?! In other words, we not only sing to him a song. We **are** to him a song! We **are** to him a praise!!

> Isa 62:6-7
> *I have set watchmen upon thy walls, O Jerusalem, which shall never hold their peace day nor night: ye that make mention of the LORD, keep not silence, And give him no rest, till he establish, and till he make Jerusalem a praise in the earth.*
>
> Jer 13:11
> *For as the girdle cleaveth to the loins of a man, so have I caused to cleave unto me the whole house of Israel and the whole house of Judah, saith the LORD; that they might be unto me for a people, and for a name, and for a praise, and for a glory...*

Jer 33:8-9
And I will cleanse them from all their iniquity, whereby they have sinned against me; and I will pardon all their iniquities, whereby they have sinned, and whereby they have transgressed against me. And it shall be to me a name of joy, a praise and an honour before all the nations of the earth, which shall hear all the good that I do unto them: and they shall fear and tremble for all the goodness and for all the prosperity that I procure unto it.

Zep 3:20
At that time will I bring you again, even in the time that I gather you: for I will make you a name and a praise among all people of the earth, when I turn back your captivity before your eyes, saith the LORD.

Throughout the scriptures, we see the word *praise*, in the English translation. But if we were to study the scriptures in the Hebrew, we would see that this word *praise* is, in actuality, many different words, with many different meanings. If we exhausted all the Hebrew words, along with their corresponding scriptures, this book would be, at best, hundreds of pages long. However, below, I've listed 10 of them, and with each one, a corresponding scripture:

(1) Todah (pron. to-daw') to offer Thanksgiving (with effort/struggle)
Psa 100:4a ° *Enter into his gates with* **thanksgiving**.

(2) Yadah (pron yaw-daw') to lift the hands (with less effort)
Psa 107:21 ° *Oh that men would* **praise** *the LORD for his goodness, and for his wonderful works to the children of men!*

(3) Halal (pron. haw-lal') to celebrate (struggle over!/beginning to enjoy)
Psa 150:6 ° *Let everything that hath breath* **praise** *the LORD.* **Praise** *ye The Lord.*

(4) Shabach (pron. shaw-bakh') to glory & triumph over
Psa 63:3 ° *Because thy lovingkindness is better than life, my lips shall* **praise** *thee.*

(5) Zamar (pron. zaw-mar') to accompany w/strings
Psa 149:3b ° *Let them* **sing praises** *unto him with the timbrel and harp.*

(6) Barak (pron. baw-rak') to kneel before & bless
Psa 103:1 ° **Bless** *the Lord, O my soul: and all that is within me,* **bless** *his holy name.*

(7) Tehillah (pron. teh-hil-law') to sing continually in the spirit
  Psa 34:1b ° *His **praise** shall continually be in my mouth.*

(8) Alatz (pron. aw-lats') to jump for joy
  Psa 9:2 ° *I will be glad and **rejoice** in You.*

(9) Ranan/Rinnah (pron. raw-nan';rin-naw') to shreak/shout for joy
  Psa 5:11 ° *But let all those that put their trust in thee rejoice: let them ever **shout** for joy.*

(10) Samach (pron. saw-makh') to be glad
  Psa 118:24 ° *This is the day which the Lord hath made; We will rejoice and be **glad** in it*

The great Bible teacher, Dr. Miles Munroe, says that there are two times when we should praise the Lord:
> (1) when we feel like it, and...
> (2) when we don't

Keeping this in mind, when God bids us to PRAISE him, there is no room for excuses. There is no room for complaints. There is not room for procrastination. There is only room for obedience!

But before we begin to praise him, we must first ask God how he wants us to praise him. We may assume that he wants us to stand and lift our hands, when, in fact, he wants us to kneel. And again, we may assume he wants us to kneel, when, in fact, he wants us to prostrate ourselves before him. Or we may want to offer thanksgiving quietly, when God wants us to praise him loudly. Or we may be doing a war cry, when God wants us to sing to him a love song.

When we truly begin to search out the scriptures and study them, we will begin to find their deeper and truer meaning. Psalms 42:7 asserts, "The deep calleth unto deep..."

2 Timothy 2:15 so aptly declares, "Study to shew thyself approved unto God, a workman that needeth not to be ashamed, rightly dividing the word of truth."

God, speaking through the prophet Jeremiah, (Jer 29:13-14), says:
  And ye shall seek me, and find me, when ye shall search for me with all your heart. And I will be found of you, saith the LORD.

Those who really desire to know the Father, must begin to press into him, until you find out what he wants; and then begin to praise him in that manner……..how **he** wants to be praised!

Let's look at one more scripture. It is Psalms 22:3 (the one we opened with).

"But thou art holy, O thou that inhabitest the praises of Israel."

The word *inhabitest*, comes from the Hebrew word *yashab* (pron. yaw-shab'), and means to sit down (or in the midst of) as judge; it also means to dwell, live in, remain, settle, or marry. The Hebrew word used here for *praises*, is the word *Tehillah*, (number 7 in the list on page 30).

So, what David is saying here, is that when we praise God to the point where we're continually singing in the spirit (where there is a residual song of praise that we hear singing deep within our members), and to the point that we walk with this song, talk with it, wake up with it, eat with it, take a bath with it, drive with it, even work with it…then **that's** the level of praise that God will dwell in, live in, or settle in. That's the type of praise that God will delight in marrying (uniting or linking up with; tying himself to). It is the only level of praise that God will inhale. It is also the only level of praise that God will sit in the midst of…on his throne...judging our circumstances and situations. It is the level of praise where God moves greatly on our behalf, meeting our needs.

When we, his people, follow this divine mandate, he has promised us that he would… "inhabit the praises of his people". ■

Chapter 7
Worship

Oh come, let us worship and bow down; Let us kneel before the LORD our Maker. (Psa 95:6)

We discovered in Chapter 6, that praise is celebration **to** God and **about** God for what he has done, what he is doing, and what he is able to do for us in the future. We also learned that Praise is concerned with God's character as well as his glorious and wonderful acts toward us, his children. And we learned that praise benefits us, not God. And lastly, we learned that God doesn't need our praise, but that we need to praise him.

However, unlike its counterpart, Praise, Worship is located in an area called "eternity". How do I know this? Well, I'm glad that you asked. Have you noticed that when you are in true worship, it seems like only minutes, when sometimes it is actually hours? And other times, when you think that you've been worshiping God for hours, it has only been minutes. It is because you are in an "eternal" moment, with no beginning and no end.

Worship is generally classified as hand lifting, kneeling, laying prostrate, bowing, basking, etc...

Matthew Henry's commentary, speaking of Cain and Abel's offering to God (discussion of Gen 4:3-5), says, "Religious Worship is not a novel invention, but an ancient institution." It has always been and will always be. "In the beginning was God...", and Worship was with God. I believe that Worship is not only an ancient institution, but also an eternal institution. It has always been, and will always be.

When God gave Moses the pattern for the Tabernacle, he made provisions so that he could meet with man. God has always wanted to fellowship with the one whom he has created in his image.

Exodus 25:21-22 describes this meeting place:

And thou shalt put the mercy seat above upon the ark...And there I will meet with thee, and I will commune with thee from above the mercy seat, from between the two cherubims which are upon the ark of the testimony, of all things which I will give thee in commandment unto the children of Israel.

One of the job functions of Aaron (high priest), as he ministered in the Tabernacle, was to burn incense upon the altar in the Holy Place (Exo 30:1, 6-8):

> *And thou shalt make an altar to burn incense upon: of shittim wood shalt thou make it. And thou shalt put it before the vail that is by the ark of the testimony, before the mercy seat that is over the testimony, where I will meet with thee. And Aaron shall burn thereon sweet incense every morning: when he dresseth the lamps, he shall burn incense upon it. And when Aaron lighteth the lamps at even, he shall burn incense upon it, a perpetual incense before the LORD throughout your generations.*

As high priest, he would take a handful of this incense and sprinkle it on the living coals on the altar. It would permeate the veil and his clothing with the fragrance of the sacrificial incense.

This represents our praise by faith. Our will, not our emotions dictate our praise in the Holy Place. But as our mind follows suit, we begin to sense overwhelming emotion. The willing praise of our lips and our heart... thrusts us forward to the point or place that brings us through the veil...into the act of worship. This is where our "sweet smelling" fragrance is received into God's very nostrils, making him well pleased with our "sacrifice"

Remember in Chapter 3, we discussed Abraham's unwavering faith in being willing to offer up (or sacrifice) his only son, Isaac, to God? Let's revisit this passage (Gen 22:2-8):

> Take now thy son, thine only son Isaac, whom thou lovest, and get thee into the land of Moriah; and offer him there for a burnt offering upon one of the mountains which I will tell thee of. And Abraham rose up early in the morning, and saddled his ass, and took two of his young men with him, and Isaac his son, and clave the wood for the burnt offering, and rose up, and went unto the place of which God had told him. Then on the third day Abraham lifted up his eyes, and saw the place afar off. And Abraham said unto his young men, Abide ye here with the ass; and *I and the lad will go yonder and worship*, and come again to you. And Abraham took the wood of the burnt offering, and laid it upon Isaac his son; and he took the fire in his hand, and a knife; and they went both of them together. And Isaac spake unto Abraham his father, and said, My father: and he said, Here am I, my son. And he said, Behold the fire and the wood: but where is the lamb for a burnt offering? And Abraham said, My son, *God will provide himself a lamb* for a burnt offering: so they went both of them together. (Italics mine)

When we praise, we are seeking God's presence. Our flesh dies willingly on the "altar of sacrifice", so that it will be a sweet smelling savor in the Father's nostrils.

Worship has nothing to do with the "flesh". It is the point where God inhabits our praise. He inhales our willing sacrifice, and we are found by him. Therefore, it is not about us at that point, but totally about Him. Only God's presence initiates worship. Remember, I said that Worship is located in the area called "Eternity"? And when you are in true worship, minutes become hours, and hours become minutes. You are in an ever glorious…."present"!

A perfect example of this "eternal moment," is the story of one of the early pioneers of the Pentecostal movement. It is the story of Maria (pron. Mah'-ree-ah) Woodworth Etter. Mrs. Etter's ministry spanned from the moment she gave her first sermon in 1879, until her death in 1924. Her home base was located in Indianapolis, Indiana; however, her ministry took her all over the United States, with thousands healed, saved, and delivered.

The story is told that once during a tent revival, Mrs. Etter was preaching. She raised her hand in order to stress a point, and went into a trance. This trance lasted for three days. Long lines of people strode by her, witnessing this miracle. For three whole days, she was transfixed with her eyes wide open. All of her bodily functions had ceased. When she came out of the trance, on the third day, she finished the point that she was making. To everyone else, it had been three days. However, to Mrs. Etter, there was no time lost at all from the beginning of that sentence, until its end!

We perfect our cooking skills, baking skills, speaking skills, and our appearance, etc… But we are missing it in the area of worship. Less than ten percent of our churches enter into true worship. We should be perfecting it, because it is the only thing that we'll be doing throughout all eternity.

Revelations 4:8-11, and 5:11-14 depict this eternal worship:

> *And the four beasts had each of them six wings about him; and they were full of eyes within: and they rest not day and night, saying, Holy, holy, holy, Lord God Almighty, which was, and is, and is to come. And when those beasts give glory and honour and thanks to him that sat on the throne, who liveth for ever and ever, The four and twenty elders fall down before him that sat on the throne, and worship him that liveth for ever and ever, and cast their crowns before the throne, saying, Thou art worthy, O Lord, to receive glory and honour and power: for thou hast created all things, and for thy pleasure they are and were created…And I beheld, and I heard the voice of many angels round about the throne and the beasts and the elders: and the number of them was ten thousand times ten thousand, and thousands of thousands; Saying with a loud voice, Worthy is the Lamb that was slain to receive power, and riches, and wisdom, and strength, and honour, and glory, and blessing. And*

every creature which is in heaven, and on the earth, and under the earth, and such as are in the sea, and all that are in them, heard I saying, Blessing, and honour, and glory, and power, be unto him that sitteth upon the throne, and unto the Lamb for ever and ever. And the four beasts said, Amen. And the four and twenty elders fell down and worshipped him that liveth for ever and ever.

The Enemy (Satan), will tolerate thanksgiving and praise, but will not tolerate worship. Satan launches an all-out attack against true worshipers. He doesn't mind the Entertainers, Pretenders, or Imitators. He doesn't mind you "…having a form of Godliness." But he hates the true Worshiper. Why? It is because thanksgiving and praise are more physical…fleshly. Satan is all about the flesh. As long as flesh is on parade, the Enemy will tolerate it. But he doesn't like it when you allow your flesh to die, and your aroma enters the Father's nostrils. Why? It is then that Father will remember you, and meet all of your needs. (Remember the Enemy comes to…"kill, to steal, and to destroy". So, he definitely doesn't want to see you blessed, nor see you get your needs met.)

I wrote a song, years ago, and the first verse went something like this:

> **The Search Is Over**
>
> I longed for something more, something that would last
> Hoping, still searching, needing healing from the past
>
> Then you spoke peace to me, healing all the hurt inside of me
> Then you showed love to me, love I'd never known, never seen
> From despair, I now have hope; from the past, I am now free
> Now the search is over, you found me

This is my point: Psalms 22:3 says, "But thou art holy, O thou that inhabitest the praises (tehillah) of Israel."

The word, *inhabit(est)*, here, is the Hebrew word *yashab* (pronounce yaw-shab') and means to live in, dwell in, occupy, reside, abide, to keep house, to settle (in or down) permanently, or remain.

Remember, we todah, yadah, halal, shabach, barak, and zamar God. All this time, we're seeking God. Barak is the crest of the wave, but we're still seeking God. However, when we begin to tehillah him, he inhales it. At the point where he inhales it, we are found of him. And when he fully consumes our tehillah, he sits in it, and makes it his permanent dwelling place.

I have heard that one of the Japanese translations of this scripture is, "When we truly praise (tehillah) God, we build a big chair for him to come and sit in."

In our praise, we are searching for him. We invite him to come and we "prepare him room".

Then he comes, and sits comfortably in our praise, transitioning it into Worship. Therefore, all of the sacrifice and struggle it takes to reach Tehillah praise, is well worth it. Because, when we tehillah God, the "Search Is Over", for….he has found us!

As a boy, David perfected worship by singing songs of praise and songs of worship to and about the Lord. The only captive audience was his father's sheep. Accompanying him, would be a harp or a flute. He would spend those long nights displaying his passionate love for his God, singing tehillah and worshiping him under the stars.

Now, let's look at Genesis 22:1-5 one more time:

And it came to pass after these things, that God did tempt Abraham, and said unto him, Abraham: and he said, Behold, here I am. And he said, Take now thy son, thine only son Isaac, whom thou lovest, and get thee into the land of Moriah; and offer him there for a burnt offering upon one of the mountains which I will tell thee of. And Abraham rose up early in the morning, and saddled his ass, and took two of his young men with him, and Isaac his son, and clave the wood for the burnt offering, and rose up, and went unto the place of which God had told him. Then on the third day Abraham lifted up his eyes, and saw the place afar off. And Abraham said unto his young men, Abide ye here with the ass; and I and the lad will go yonder and worship, and come again to you.

Abraham didn't call it "sacrifice", he called it "worship"! They were one in the same to him. Because of his covenant with God, he knew that God would meet him there, therefore he said, "God will provide himself a lamb." His covenant partner had to show up. His "presence" would be there!

Let's take a look at a few Hebrew words. This will give us a deeper understanding of what it means to worship.

The Hebrew word for *worship,* used here, is the word *shachah* (pronounced shaw-khaw'), and means to stoop or crouch down, to lower oneself-or to lay prostrate making obeisance, humbly beseeching the Lord.

In Psalms 95, we see this word again. Here, David instructs the people of God to come, sing unto the Lord, and make a joyful noise unto their God, the great King. He encourages them to come before his presence with thanksgiving. And then he says in verse 6:

> Oh come, let us *worship* and *bow down*; Let us *kneel* before the LORD our Maker.

Let's take a closer look at this to find out just what David is saying.

The Hebrew word, used here again, is *shachah*. The word, *worship*, is joined by another term, *bow down*, which is the Hebrew word, *kara* (pronounce kawrah'). Kara has similar meaning; It means to sink or cast oneself down; to bend the knee. It also means to fall down prostrate. And, of course, we've already defined what barak means.

So when we put it all together, here's what David was really saying:

> Oh come, let us stoop or crouch down. Let us lower ourselves making obeisance, humbly beseeching the Lord. Let us bend our knees, sinking and falling prostrate; Let us pay tribute to Him in loyal indebtedness. Let us wait before the LORD our Maker, in great expectation.

Let's look at a few more scriptures that use this Hebrew word *shachah*. The first is Nehemiah 9:5-6:

> *And the Levites, Jeshua, Kadmiel, Bani, Hashabniah, Sherebiah, Hodijah, Shebaniah, and Pethahiah, said: Stand up and bless the LORD your God Forever and ever! Blessed be Your glorious name, Which is exalted above all blessing and praise! You alone are the LORD; You have made heaven, The heaven of heavens, with all their host, The earth and everything on it, The seas and all that is in them, And You preserve them all. The host of heaven worships (shachah) You. (Par. mine.)*

The Ark of God had been taken by the Philistines. When David bought the Ark of Covenant back into the City of David (1 Chr 16), included are these words to the psalm that he wrote for the celebration:

> *Give unto the LORD the glory due unto his name: bring an offering, and come before him: worship the LORD in the beauty of holiness.*

In Psalms 22:27, David proclaims, "All the ends of the world shall remember and turn unto the LORD: and all the kindreds of the nations shall worship before thee." And in Psalm 66:4, the psalmist declares, "All the earth shall worship thee, and shall sing unto thee; they shall sing to thy name. Selah."

In Psalms 99:5 and 9, the psalmist commands us saying:

Exalt ye the LORD our God, and worship at his footstool; for he is holy. Exalt the LORD our God, and worship at his holy hill; for the LORD our God is holy.

In Psalms 132:7, he asserts, "We will go into his tabernacles: we will worship at his footstool." And in Psalms 138:2 he affirms, "I will worship toward thy holy temple, and praise thy name for thy lovingkindness and for thy truth: for thou hast magnified thy word above all thy name."

Worship, in another way, means simply to abandon yourself totally and willingly, submitting to God, your Lord and Master. I like to say that worship is an attitude, or posture (position inward and outward) toward God. When we worship God, we focus our affection on him only. We are with him right where he is, and we "behold His glory" (John 17:24). In other words, we fix, make firm, establish, secure, immobilize, put in order, settle permanently, or gaze our eyes and our attention fully and undeniably on him; nothing and no-one else matters, but him.

"Flesh" is nowhere in sight; for you see, it has been left in the realm called "Time"; but once the eternal God inhabits our praise, there is an exchange; as I said earlier, God's very presence initiates worship. Since worship lies in an eternal realm, only an eternal God can grant us entrance (by way of the spirit) into it.

Worship is from the heart of God, to the heart of God. It is that that presses into God, until it taps into what he wants, and then that's what you give, do, or say back to him. The goal is to worship past flesh until God sits in the room; and when God sits in the room, needs are met.

Remember, we discussed in the last chapter how David understood that to truly sacrifice something to the Lord should cost you? It's not a sacrifice unless it holds great value to you.

That is why God had the Israelites raise a lamb in Egypt for the Passover. He wanted them to get to know this lamb. This lamb became a part of the family. They fed it. They played with it. They kept it close to them. They knew its sound above all the other family's lamb. They got very attached to this little lamb. But during Passover, they would have to sacrifice this creature that had become like a "family pet" to them. God wanted them to value that lamb, so that they would know the cost of true sacrifice (symbolic of the Father sacrifice of his most precious son!)

We also discussed in the last chapter, how Mary, the sister of Lazarus, broke open her valuable alabaster box of precious perfumed oil, and anointed Jesus with it.

She counted the cost to know him…to worship him, and it was well worth every cent (and much more!), than that oil had cost her.

In John 4:23-24, Jesus reveals the heart of the Father concerning worship, and the true worshipers of which he is seeking:

> *But the hour cometh, and now is, when the true worshippers shall worship the Father in spirit and in truth: for the Father seeketh such to worship him. God is a Spirit: and they that worship him must worship him in spirit and in truth.* ■

O The Glory

O the glory of your presence, we embrace
As we wait for you, O Lord, come fill this place

As we worship you, Your Majesty
We bow on bended knee
As we give to you all honor and praise
As your presence now fills this place

Chapter 8
The Cost of Worship

And the king said...I will surely buy it of thee at a price: neither will I offer burnt offerings unto the LORD my God of that which doth cost me nothing. (2Sam 24:24)

Exodus Chapter 24 records that Moses was called up into Mount Sinai, by God, where he showed him the pattern of how to build and furnish the Tabernacle. It was to be prepared by his exact specifications.

In Exodus 25:2-8, the Lord speaks to Moses, and says:
> *Speak unto the children of Israel, that they bring me an offering: of every man that giveth it willingly with his heart ye shall take my offering. And this is the offering which ye shall take of them; gold, and silver, and brass, And blue, and purple, and scarlet, and fine linen, and goats' hair, And rams' skins dyed red, and badgers' skins, and shittim wood, Oil for the light, spices for anointing oil, and for sweet incense, Onyx stones, and stones to be set in the ephod, and in the breastplate. And let them make me a sanctuary; that I may dwell among them.*

This tabernacle was to be elaborate. No expense was to be spared. After all, this is where the Supreme Magistrate-Exceeding All Else, and the Self Existent-Eternal God was to dwell. It was to cost the Israelite's something. But whatever the cost, it was to be given willingly.

In the Most Holy Place (or the Holiest), there were to be two articles: (1) the Ark of Covenant, and (2) the Mercy Seat. The Ark of Covenant was to be made of a specific wood (shittum), and then overlaid with gold. The Mercy Seat (and the Cherubim affixed to it) was to be made of pure gold.

In the Holy place, there were to be three articles: (1) the Table of Shewbread, (2) the Golden Candlestick, and (3) the Golden Altar of Incense. The Table of Shewbread was to be made of Shittum wood and overlaid with gold. The Golden Candlestick was not to be made of hollowed gold, but was to be made of solid gold throughout. And the Golden Altar of Incense was to be made of Shittum wood and overlaid with gold.

So, you see, this was a very expensive undertaking. This is the place where the Israelite's would praise their God. This is the place where God would tabernacle with them.

Some people have said that it costs you nothing to worship the Lord. I beg to differ. It costs you your flesh, your will, your heart, your mind, your possessions, and your very life! It will cost you...EVERYTHING!!! No. Worship is **not** free!

Let's look and see what it cost David.

In 2 Samuel chapter 24, we have the account in which David (out of the pride of his heart) sends the captain of the host (Joab) to number Israel and Judah. Joab, voices his opposition to it, but nevertheless obeys his king.

You see, God wanted David's full-fledged faith in him. He wanted David to believe that he was Jehovah Malak (Jehovah who reigns victoriously) and Jehovah Yeshua (Jehovah who saves and delivers whether by many of by few). David's numbering the people showed a lack of trust in God's ability.

But here is why God said that David was a man after his own heart. 2 Samuel 24:10 says:

> *And David's heart smote him after that he had numbered the people. And David said unto the LORD, I have sinned greatly in that I have done: and now, I beseech thee, O LORD, take away the iniquity of thy servant; for I have done very foolishly.*

David's heart was pricked, and his conscience revealed to him the evil that he had committed. Quickly, he admitted his sin (that'll preach, right there!), and asked God to take away the iniquity of this foolish thing that he had done, by numbering the people. But as a result of his anger, God offered David a choice between these three things: (1) seven years of famine, (2) to flee three months before his enemies, while they pursued him, or (3) three days' pestilence in the land.

I love David's response (2 Sam 24:14):

> *And David said unto Gad, I am in a great strait: let us fall now into the hand of the LORD; for his mercies are great: and let me not fall into the hand of man.*

David knew from experience, that the Lord was great and plenteous in mercy. He knew that God knew his own people, and what they could stand. He trusted that the Lord would choose the better of the 3 choices.

Let's look at the merciful choice God makes for David. It is found, here, in the next two verses:

> *So the LORD sent a pestilence upon Israel from the morning even to the time appointed: and there died of the people from Dan even to Beersheba seventy thousand men. And when the angel stretched out his hand upon Jerusalem to destroy it, the LORD repented him of the evil, and said to the angel that destroyed the people, It is enough: stay now thine hand. And the angel of the LORD was by the threshingplace of Araunah the Jebusite.*

Stay with me. We're getting closer to the point of the matter.

Now, the prophet, Gad, tells David to erect an altar in Araunah's threashingfloor. In obedience, David goes to do so.

Araunah look's out and sees David and his servants coming his way. He runs out to greet him, and bowing down he exclaims, *"Wherefore is my lord the king come to his servant?"* Let's follow the rest of their conversation (2 Sam 24:21b -23):

> *And David said, To buy the threshingfloor of thee, to build an altar unto the LORD, that the plague may be stayed from the people. And Araunah said unto David, Let my lord the king take and offer up what seemeth good unto him: behold, here be oxen for burnt sacrifice, and threshing instruments and other instruments of the oxen for wood. All these things did Araunah, as a king, give unto the king. And Araunah said unto the king, The LORD thy God accept thee.*

David's response is my key point (verse 24):

> *And the king said unto Araunah, Nay; but I will surely buy it of thee at a price: neither will I offer burnt offerings unto the LORD my God of that which doth cost me nothing.*

If it doesn't cost you anything, then it holds no value or worth to you. You will not truly appreciate what has been done for you. Let me give you three examples:

(1) Your son, Jamie, has been raised knowing that everything that he asks for will be given to him. Therefore, that new sweater that you've just bought him, will probably be thrown on the floor, rather than hung up properly. Why? It's just another sweater, to him.

(2) That new telephone may be haphazardly left somewhere, without any concern to him. Why? Because he knows that you will give him another one.

(3) You bought him a brand new baseball glove, this week. It will probably be left out in the yard...in the rain, a couple of times this week. Why? It's ..."just a glove", and he knows that you'll get him another one.

Why would Jamie not take better care of these things? It's simple. They hold no worth or value, to him. It didn't cost him anything to obtain them.

But let Jamie mow lawns, or deliver papers in order to pay for that sweater, that phone, or that glove. I guarantee there'll be a different response. That sweater will hang neatly on a hanger. That phone will stay in Jamie's holster, attached to his side. And that glove will stay neatly in the place prepared for it in the corner, beside that ball and bat.

∽♥∾

"After two days was the feast of the passover, and of unleavened bread..." (Mar 14:1a)

Jesus had arrived six days before the time of the feast of the Passover and of Unleavened Bread. Mark recounts that Jesus was in Bethany at Simon the leper's house, four days later. He had decided to join him for an evening meal, two days prior to the feast.

Alright, so by now, you know I love Word study! So, you know that I couldn't resist looking up the word *Bethany*!

The Greek spelling is actually *Bethania* (pron. Bay-than-ee'-ah), and it means...date house! There was no coincidence! Everything that Jesus did, was calculated (for an intended purpose).

Let's continue with the story (Mark 14:3):
> "And being in Bethany in the house of Simon the leper, as he sat at meat, there came a woman having an alabaster box of ointment of spikenard very precious; and she brake the box, and poured it on his head."

John 11:2 verifies that this Mary, and Lazarus' sister, Mary, were one in the same. Luke's account starts out similar (Luke 7:37), but adds in verse 38, that she "...stood at his feet behind him weeping, and began to wash his feet with tears, and did wipe them with the hairs of her head, and kissed his feet, and anointed them with the ointment."

The Greek word for *spikenard* is *nardos pistikos* (pron. nar'-dos pis-tik-os'), and means genuine, unadulterated or pure nard (myrrh or fragrant ointment).

Let's look at the importance of this oil. Let's look at Exodus 30:22-25, and 35:

> *Moreover the LORD spake unto Moses, saying, Take thou also unto thee principal spices, of pure myrrh five hundred shekels, and of sweet cinnamon half so much, even two hundred and fifty shekels, and of sweet calamus two hundred and fifty shekels, And of cassia five hundred shekels, after the shekel of the sanctuary, and of oil olive an hin: And thou shalt make it an oil of holy ointment, an ointment compound after the art of the apothecary: it shall be an holy anointing oil...And thou shalt make it a perfume, a confection after the art of the apothecary, tempered together, pure and holy:*

This oil was originally so important that it was not to be used on anyone but the priests. No one could make any oil like it. And it obviously had a pleasing odor because the Israelites were charged not even make it for the express purpose of smelling its perfume. If they copied its composition, they would be cut off from the people!

This myrrh that Mary possessed, was worth over $300 pence, and was well over a year's wages. However, the cost of it meant nothing to her, in comparison to what Jesus had done for her. He had opened up the Gospel to her, making her aware of her sins. And sorrowful for these sins, and with thanksgiving and praise in her heart, she had now come...and had worshiped him.

Some of the disciples were filled with righteous indignation at what they perceived as a waste of money. However, Jesus responded by saying that none of them had done for him what she had done.

He concluded the matter by saying (Luke 7:47-48 & 50):

> *Wherefore I say unto thee, Her sins, which are many, are forgiven; for she loved much: but to whom little is forgiven, the same loveth little. And he said unto her, Thy sins are forgiven...And he said to the woman, Thy faith hath saved thee; go in peace.*

There is an old hymn, and its chorus goes something like this:

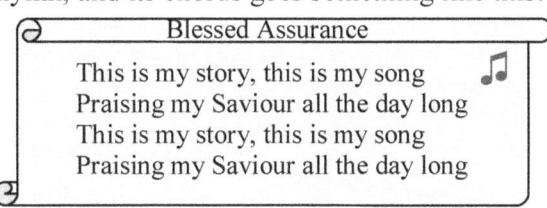

I have a friend who says, "If you don't know my story, you won't understand my praise! You won't understand my worship!!!"

In other words, if you don't know what I've been through (deliverance from drugs, alcohol, psychological problems, poverty, adultery, fornication, sickness, disease, rejection, abuse, death, etc...), then you won't understand why I sing, jump, shout, clap my hands, cry, spin around, sing, dance, laugh, bow down, lift my hands, or lay prostrate when I feel the overwhelming power of God.

In Matthew 26:12-13, Jesus closes the matter by declaring:

For in that she hath poured this ointment on my body, she did it for my burial. Verily I say unto you, Wheresoever this gospel shall be preached in the whole world, there shall also this, that this woman hath done, be told for a memorial of her.

Jesus had made a *date* with destiny! This encounter would fulfill a dual purpose:

   (1) Mary would receive forgiveness of sins, and
   (2) Jesus would be anointed for burial.

Psalm 51:17 declares, "The sacrifices of God are a broken spirit: a broken and a contrite (to break sore) heart, O God, thou wilt not despise (count as insignificant)." (parentheses mine) Psalm 34b says, he "...saveth such as be of a contrite spirit."

That ointment that Mary poured on Jesus cost her a year's wages. But what she got, in return, was much, much more than she could have ever imagined. (1) She learned how to truly worship the Master in sweet abandon, (2) Her sins were forgiven her, and (3) for over 2000 years she has been remembered, and will continue to be, as long as the Gospel is preached. (I'd say she made a wise investment!)

In 1983, I was privileged to go to the country of Pakistan. I was guest to a missionary who represented the United Presbyterian Church, there.

One of the events, that would help to shape my life forever, happened one night at a convention to which we were invited. The convention was called The Sialkot Convention, and was held in Sialkot, a few hours away. This convention had been founded by the Apostle John Hyde (1904), and two friends and I were to minister there in song, and share our testimonies. We, being very excited for the opportunity, sang and shared passionately about our Lord and Saviour.

At the end of service, a young girl came up at the invitation. She said that she was a Muslim. But because of my testimony, she was ready to turn from Allah, and give her heart to Jesus, the true Messiah. She went on to say:

> Now, you must understand, that as of this very moment, I've committed treason in my country. And by morning, my parents will go to the national archives and wipe out my name. It will be as though I was never born; I now have no country. But because of your testimony, I believe that Jesus is the true Messiah, the Son of the Living God.

And she said further:

> You must also understand, that as one that has committed treason, I am now an outlaw, and my family will hire killers to take my life. But because of your testimony, I believe that Jesus is the true Messiah, the Son of the Living God.

She said one last thing:

> And you must understand that as of this moment, I have no home to go to, for my parents have now disowned me. I am only 16, so you must pray that a family will take me in, tonight. But because of your testimony, I believe that Jesus is the true Messiah, the Son of the Living God.

Now, up until that point, I really thought that I had counted the cost of having the opportunity to freely worship God. But I still had my mother and father, sisters and brothers, and material things (cars, money, home, etc...) But, I had truly learned what it was to forsake all (Matt 10:27; 19:29; Mar 10:29-30), from this 16 year old Pakistani Muslim girl.

That night, I made an altar at the end of my bed, and "what things were gain to me, those I counted loss for Christ." (Phi 3:7)

Remember, worship will cost you. But also remember, that whatever the cost, it can never match the return that God will give to you. No matter the cost, it is the wisest investment you will ever make; for you are in an unequal covenant. Whatever it has and will cost you, it cost him more! ■

Chapter 9
The Role of the Congregation in Worship

O praise the LORD, all ye nations: praise him, all ye people....Praise ye the LORD. (Psa 117:1-2)

In Psalms 122:1, David proclaims, "I was glad when they said unto me, Let us go into the house of the LORD."

David had learned to find solace and protection in the house of the Lord. There, he would worship the Lord, experiencing sweet fellowship with him. Sometimes he would speak to God. Sometimes God would speak to him. And at other times, David would just sit in God's presence in silence. Through his humble beginnings as a shepherd boy (worshiping God in the pasture, and in these private temple sessions with the Lord), David grew to know the Father's heart. In Acts 13:22, Paul recounts the story regarding David, saying:

> ...he (God) raised up unto them David to be their king; to whom also he gave testimony, and said, I have found David the son of Jesse, a man after mine own heart, which shall fulfil all my will. (Parentheses mine)

Although he loved these private moments with his God, he never failed to worship in the great assembly. David had experienced God in those private sessions, but he also believed in the corporate celebration of worship. For in it, he saw the majesty and greatness of God displayed on a different magnitude. He saw God's love for his people on display.

In Psalms 96:1-9, David commands the congregation, saying:

> O sing unto the LORD a new song: sing unto the LORD, all the earth. Sing unto the LORD, bless his name; shew forth his salvation from day to day. Declare his glory among the heathen, his wonders among all people. For the LORD is great, and greatly to be praised: he is to be feared above all gods. For all the gods of the nations are idols: but the LORD made the heavens. Honour and majesty are before him: strength and beauty are in his sanctuary. Give unto the LORD, O ye kindreds of the people, give unto the LORD glory and strength. Give unto the LORD the glory due unto his name: bring an offering, and come into his courts. O worship the LORD in the beauty of holiness: fear before him, all the earth.

The Hebrew word for *sanctuary* is *miqdash* [f] (pron. mik-dawsh'), or *miqedash* [m] (pron. mik-ked-awsh'), and means a consecrated place, or a place of asylum (safety or refuge.)

David is saying that we are to come together, singing new songs to the Lord, blessing his name, declaring his greatness, honor, glory, and majesty. And as we give the Lord what is due him, he will empower us so that we can go out into the highways and byways, and publish the good news of his saving power. We are to tell of his wonders...both to our fellow congregant, and to the heathen. He reminds the congregation that strength (boldness) and beauty (bravery) are found in God's holy place of refuge...in the place of safety. He bids us to offer up praises to him and draw near to him, worshiping him in the beauty of holiness.

Let me give you an example of this.

Some years ago, I was invited to York, England to minister. This church is situated near the center of town. Around the corner, from this church, is an area that they call "The Strip". Located on both sides of this "Strip", is around forty bars. It is a "hot spot" for young college students, who come from miles around just to drink at these bars. They arrive on Friday night, and try to drink in as many bars as they can. Then, they return on Saturday night, and do the same thing. The ultimate goal is to try and drink in all forty of them…in one night!

These bars don't only cater to college students. The owners also try to make them attractive to adults (including married couples with families), so they serve full course meals in them -as well as- alcohol.

Well, as you would imagine, this type of activity produces a scene of drunkenness and disorderly conduct on a massive scale.

(That's the backdrop. Now, let's get back to the story.)

The church that invited me, had a good idea of Kingdom Purpose. On Friday nights, they have an evening service, and the first hour and 15 minutes, is a time of intense worship.

After being empowered through this time of worship, a well-prepared ministry team goes out on "The Strip". While out there, the church goes into intercessory prayer for them. They go into the bars and invite individuals (or families) to come with them… "around the corner, for a nice time…and great music!"

Which such intensity in Worship and Prayer, the sinner's hearts are made pliable. The ministry team, brings them around the corner, to the church; and hearing the message, they come forward to surrender their lives to Jesus. Some of the men (that are out alone), have been known to go home and get their wives (and children)… bringing them back, to also give their hearts to the Lord.

The night that I was there, I witnessed, first hand, many people coming back with the team...all of them, giving their hearts to the Lord! And as they gave their hearts to the Lord, we had A.T.I.T.T. (an acronym for...A Time In The Temple), celebrating...praising God, for the wonderful salvation of souls!

This is the role of the congregation in worship. They had charged the atmosphere with their worship, which, in turn, had empowered the team to go out; and "The Lord added to the church..." (Acts 2:47).

Leviticus 26:8 says, "And five of you shall chase an hundred, and an hundred of you shall put ten thousand to flight: and your enemies shall fall before you...." Then, can you imagine the power of an entire congregation of more than seven-hundred zealous worshipers? What about the CHURCH united?!?

Below, I list 10 things, that we, as a congregation, must begin to do, when we come together to worship:

(1) Offer up thanksgiving (Psa 107:22):
And let them sacrifice the sacrifices of thanksgiving, and declare his works with rejoicing.

(2) Enter into praise (Psa 150:1):
Praise ye the LORD. Praise God in his sanctuary...

(3) Celebrate (Psa 32:11 MSG):
Celebrate GOD.
Sing together--everyone! All you honest hearts, raise the roof!

(4) Clap our hands (Psa 47:1a):
O clap your hands, all ye people...

(5) Shout (Psa 47:1b):
Shout unto God with the voice of triumph.

(6) Dance (Psa 149:3):
Let them praise his name in the dance...

(7) Make confession (Jam 5:16):
Confess your faults one to another, and pray one for another, that ye may be healed.

(8) Repent (Acts 17:30):
And the times of this ignorance God winked at; but now commandeth all men every where to repent:

(9) Forgive one another (Eph 4:32):
And be ye kind one to another, tenderhearted, forgiving one another, even as God for Christ's sake hath forgiven you.

(10) Testify (Psa 40:10):
I didn't keep the news of your ways a secret, didn't keep it to myself. I told it all, how dependable you are, how thorough. I didn't hold back pieces of love and truth For myself alone. I told it all, let the congregation know the whole story.

(11) Pray & Intercede (Psa 32:6 MSG/Acts 12:5):
Every one of us needs to pray; when all hell breaks loose and the dam bursts we'll be on high ground, untouched.

...prayer was made without ceasing of the church unto God for him.

(12) Watch over one another (Heb 10:24):
And let us consider and give attentive, continuous care to watching over one another..

(13) Encourage one another (1 The 5:11):
So speak encouraging words to one another. Build up hope so you'll all be together in this, no one left out, no one left behind. I know you're already doing this; just keep on doing it.

(14) Sing (Psa 30:4):
Sing unto the LORD, O ye saints of his, and give thanks at the remembrance of his holiness.

(15) Kneel (Psa 95:6):
O come, let us worship and bow down: let us kneel before the LORD our maker.

(16) Lay Prostrate (1 Chr 29:20):
And David said to all the congregation, Now bless the LORD your God. And all the congregation blessed the LORD God of their fathers, and bowed down their heads, and worshipped the LORD...

(17) Be quiet, and wait in his presence (Zec 2:13 MSG):
Quiet, everyone! Shh! Silence before GOD. Something's afoot in his holy house. He's on the move!

(18) Worship (Psa 95:6):
O come, let us worship and bow down: let us kneel before the LORD our maker.

(19) Love one another (Joh 13:35)
By this shall all men know that ye are my disciples, if ye have love one to another.

(20) Serve one another (Gal 5:13)
...by love serve one another.

(21) Prophesy to one another (1 Cor 14:3, 4, 24, 25):
...he that prophesieth speaketh unto men to edification, and exhortation, and comfort.

...he that prophesieth edifieth the church. But if all prophesy, and there come in one that believeth not, or one unlearned, he is convinced of all, he is judged of all: And thus are the secrets of his heart made manifest; and so falling down on his face he will worship God, and report that God is in you of a truth.

The Hebrew word for *congregation* is *qahal* (pron. kaw-hawl), and simply means assembly, company, or multitude (of people). The word, assembly, in turn, means congregation. It also means congress.

In Psalms 27:4 (AMP), David declares:
One thing have I asked of the Lord, that will I seek, inquire for, and [*insistently*] require: that I may dwell in the house of the Lord [*in His presence*] all the days of my life, to behold and gaze upon the beauty [*the sweet attractiveness and the delightful loveliness*] of the Lord and to meditate, consider, and inquire in His temple.

A congress is a formal meeting of delegates or representatives (persons who are chosen to represent -or given the authority to act on behalf of- another) to discuss matters of interest or concern.

We are delegates and representatives of the Kingdom of God. So when we gather to worship, the atmosphere is both charged and changed; and as we in-

issues and matters of concern...not only for the church, but for the world!

2 Chronicles 5:5-7, 11, 13-14, details a portion of the dedication of Solomon's temple:

> *And they brought up the ark, and the tabernacle of the congregation...Also king Solomon, and all the congregation of Israel that were assembled unto him before the ark...And they brought up the ark, and the tabernacle of the congregation, And the priests brought in the ark of the covenant of the LORD unto his place, to the oracle of the house, into the most holy place, even under the wings of the cherubims: And it came to pass, when the priests were come out of the holy place: It came even to pass, as the trumpeters and singers were as one, to make one sound to be heard in praising and thanking the LORD; and when they lifted up their voice with the trumpets and cymbals and instruments of musick, and praised the LORD, saying, For he is good; for his mercy endureth for ever: that then the house was filled with a cloud, even the house of the LORD; So that the priests could not stand to minister by reason of the cloud: for the glory of the LORD had filled the house of God.*

When the people came together as one...with the sole purpose of making one sound in praising God, **then** the cloud of the glorious presence of the Lord filled the house; so much so, the priest could not stand to minister! We should never underestimate the power of corporate Worship!!!

When we as a congregation begin to come together to make one sound in worship, and are consistent and diligent in doing this, then the heaviness of God's presence (his glory and splendor) will fill the house. And when it does, there will be confession, repentance, revival, salvation, deliverance, healing, restoration, miracles, signs, and wonders on a massive scale. ■

Below, I list 30 keys for an effective congregation:

1. Be submitted to authority. (Heb 13:17)
    a. *Obey them that have the rule over you, and submit yourselves (surrender, volunteer, extend yourself for service): for they watch for your souls, as <u>they that must give account</u>.*
2. Be willing to follow the leader, as he follows Christ.
    a. Know the Vision of your local church.
       (You can't follow a vision you don't know.
    b. Understand that the pastor sees the <u>full</u> Vision; you only see in part.
3. Be a tithe payer.
4. Have a growing relationship and fellowship with God.
5. Be a worshiper at home, learning to spend time in God's presence.
6. Spend time in preparation, prior to coming to"His House".
    a. When you arrive, your hearts will be pliable.
    b. When you arrive, your spirits will be ready to both give <u>to</u> and receive <u>from</u> God.
7. Teach your children to worship God.
8. Realize that God is listening for **ONE** united voice, when we come together in corporate worship.
9. Be quick to encourage others, keep peace; be a helper of the joy of others.
10. Strive to be freely expressive in worship as a holy example before the Body.
11. Learn to focus your affection & attention totally & completely on God.
12. Strive to be hasty to pray (especially joining in corporate prayer).
13. Strive to be hasty to give when asked (or prompted by your leader).
14. Learn to dress appropriately for worship, remembering…you represent both your leader & God.
15. Strive to be hasty to stand and praise God.
16. Strive to be hasty to fall down on your knees (or prostrate) in worship, if God so moves.
17. Learn to love and care about God's people.
18. Strive to be willing to be shabared (Hebrew for "broken"). (Psa 51:17)
19. Strive to obtain good integrity and a good moral character.
20. Strive to be servants.
21. Strive to be timely; God shows up on time to meet your needs.
    You don't want to miss Him if he so desires to do all of his "moving" at the beginning of the Worship Service.

22. Show up with an expectant spirit.
23. Strive to be quick to forgive.
24. Strive to be quick to repent.
25. Strive to be open to allow God to move...even if different from your planned program.
26. Spend time in prayer, praying for yourself and interceding for the Body.
27. Strive to be quick to listen, quick to hear, and even quicker to obey.
28. Strive to be like God: Givers
29. Learn to give God what He thinks he's worth, not what you think he is worth!
30. Realize that worship is **not** an option; it is a command!

Practice, perfect, and enjoy worship! After all, you're going to be doing it forever! ■

...the people that do know their God shall be strong, and do exploits. (Dan 11:32)

Chapter 10
A Royal Priesthood

...ye are a chosen generation, a royal priesthood, an holy nation, a peculiar people; that ye should shew forth the praises of him who hath called you out of darkness into his marvellous light... (1Pe 2:9)

Peter, in his letter to the Christians who were exiled and dispersed in Pontus, Galatia, Cappadocia, Asia, and Bithynia, was quoting (in this opening scripture) from the book of Exodus 19:5-6, where God spoke to Moses saying:

> Now therefore, if ye will obey my voice indeed, and keep my covenant, then ye shall be a peculiar treasure unto me above all people: for all the earth is mine: And ye shall be unto me a kingdom of priests, and an holy nation. These are the words which thou shalt speak unto the children of Israel.

The word in Hebrew for *peculiar treasure*, is the word *segullah* (pron. seg-oo-law'), and means to shut up (or shut off) inferring to purchase, acquire, or possess; to take for ones' self. God said that the whole earth was his, but Israel was special...his "special treasure".

The Hebrew word, here, for *kingdom*, is the word *mamlakah* (pron. mam-law-kaw'), and means dominion, power, authority, or rulership.

The Hebrew word for *priest(s)*, is the word *kohen* (pron. ko-hane'), and means officiator, acting priest, or chief ruler.

An holy nation is defined as a sanctified or sacred state, empire, kingdom, monarchy, race, or tribe.

As kingdom priests, their purpose was to be chief rulers, ruling with authority and power, subduing all the other nations, and showing forth the excellency of Jehovah God before all of the other nations of the land. And by this, all of the other nations would know that the Israelite's God reigned as the Elohiym...the supreme God...exceeding all other gods.

It was God's original plan that the entire nation of Israel be a kingdom of priests. So he began by setting up the office of priest as a type and shadow, to show us how kingdom priests should function.

After Nadab and Abihu died before the Lord (offering strange fire before him), there were only three priests left in that functioning office to serve the entire nation of Israel: Aaron (High Priest), and his two sons, Eleazar, and Ithamar.

God spoke to Moses, and told him to bring the tribe of Levi near. The Levites were then set apart from the rest of the tribe of Israel, as first fruits offered to God. They were given wholly to Aaron, the High Priest. Their purpose was to serve in the Tabernacle of the Congregation, assisting the priests in their ministration to the Lord.

Listen to what God said, concerning the Levites (Num 3:12):

And I, behold, I have taken the Levites from among the children of Israel instead of all the firstborn that openeth the matrix among the children of Israel: therefore the Levites shall be mine...

The Levites were to be set apart as the Lord's. They were to be sanctified. They were to be holy. They were to stay consecrated to God. They were to always dress appropriately, as one serving in the tabernacle where God dwelt. They were not to partake of anything unholy...anything that would displease the Lord God. They were to daily come before his presence, with sacrificial offerings. They were to offer thanksgiving offerings, sin offerings, peace offerings, and other offerings. They were to lift up prayers daily for themselves and for the people. They were to keep the altar of incense burning twenty four hours a day, symbolic of our praises (in David's tabernacle, the Levitical priests, dedicated as singers and musicians, would lift up praises unto him twenty four hours a day!). They were to function in their perspective offices with authority.

We, as citizens of the United States, don't really have a concept of KINGDOM. Our system of government is set up as a democracy. The word *democracy* means free and equal representation of the people. In a democratic nation, the government is elected freely and equally by all of its citizens. As a system of government, it is based on the principle of majority decision-making.

God never meant for there to be a democracy. His original plan has always been to have a kingdom. You always read in scripture, "The kingdom of heaven is like..," "For thine is the kingdom, and the power, and the glory..," "For the kingdom of God is not meat and drink..," "But seek ye first the kingdom of God..," or "For the kingdom of God is not in word, but in power." Everything is always likened unto a kingdom.

In Matthew 6:10, Jesus is teaching the people to pray. The third and fourth line of this model prayer reads, "Thy kingdom come. Thy will be done. In earth, as it is in heaven."

So, since heaven is established on kingdom principles, earth, then, should resemble heaven.

In a kingdom, the king rules; he owns the land. It is his responsibility to take care of his subjects. Every king wants to shine greatest before all the other kings. They want to have the largest kingdom. They want to be the most prosperous and the most celebrated king in all the earth.

When there is famine in the land, it makes the king look bad. When there is no proper housing in the land, it makes the king look bad. When there is no proper health care, who looks bad? Yes! You've guessed it…the king. Why? A good king is supposed to provide for his subjects. They should not have a care in the world. Every subject should be able to rest at night, knowing that his king has his best interest at heart. If anybody is burning the midnight oil…it should be the king.

In Revelations 11:15, John records these words:

> *And the seventh angel sounded; and there were great voices in heaven, saying, The kingdoms of this world are become the kingdoms of our Lord, and of his Christ; and he shall reign for ever and ever.*

When we, as Christians, get back to being Kingdom minded, we will begin to function as true kings and priests. And when all is said and done, there'll be no more patterns of the heavenly kingdom. The kingdom of God will be established on earth with Christ as the King of kings, and the Lord of lords!

Let's look at our opening scripture (1Pet 2:9) one more time:

> *But ye are a chosen generation, a royal priesthood, an holy nation, a peculiar people; that ye should shew forth the praises of him who hath called you out of darkness into his marvellous light…*

Now let's decipher it:

We are to be a selected and preferred generation. We are to be God's prized possession, purchased and acquired through the shed blood of Jesus Christ. We are also to be a sanctified and sacred empire of people; a kingdom…a monarchy.

We are not to be a "normal" priesthood, but greater than that; a royal or kingly priesthood. We are priesthood that shows off our majestic, splendid, grandiose, magnificent, and superb God.

We are to look like royalty, walk like royalty, talk like royalty, think like royalty, live like royalty, worship like royalty, and conduct business like royalty.

Our purpose, as kingdom priests, is to make known (through celebration) the excellence of our God. Why? He has delivered us from obscurity, and placed us into his manifested presence.

Let's close with the entire second chapter of Peter. I think that it gives us godly direction on how we should conduct ourselves as a royal priesthood.

1Peter 2:1-21, 24-25 (AMP)

> SO BE done with every trace of wickedness (depravity, malignity) and all deceit and insincerity (pretense, hypocrisy) and grudges (envy, jealousy) and slander and evil speaking of every kind. Like newborn babies you should crave (thirst for, earnestly desire) the pure (unadulterated) spiritual milk, that by it you may be nurtured and grow unto [*completed*] salvation, Since you have [*already*] tasted the goodness and kindness of the Lord. [*Ps. 34:8.*] Come to Him [*then, to that*] Living Stone which men tried and threw away, but which is chosen [*and*] precious in God's sight. [*Ps. 118:22; Isa. 28:16.*] [*Come*] and, like living stones, be yourselves built [*into*] a spiritual house, for a holy (dedicated, consecrated) priesthood, to offer up [*those*] spiritual sacrifices [*that are*] acceptable and pleasing to God through Jesus Christ. For thus it stands in Scripture: Behold, I am laying in Zion a chosen (honored), precious chief Cornerstone, and he who believes in Him [*who adheres to, trusts in, and relies on Him*] shall never be disappointed or put to shame. [*Isa. 28:16.*] To you then who believe (who adhere to, trust in, and rely on Him) is the preciousness; but for those who disbelieve [*it is true*], The [*very*] Stone which the builders rejected has become the main Cornerstone, [*Ps. 118:22.*] And, A Stone that will cause stumbling and a Rock that will give [*men*] offense; they stumble because they disobey and disbelieve [*God's*] Word, as those [*who reject Him*] were destined (appointed) to do. But you are a chosen race, a royal priesthood, a dedicated nation, [*God's*] own purchased, special people, that you may set forth the wonderful deeds and display the virtues and perfections of Him Who called you out of darkness into His marvelous light. [*Exod. 19:5, 6.*] Once you were not a people [*at all*], but now you are God's people; once you were unpitied, but now you are pitied and have received mercy. [*Hos. 2:23.*] Beloved, I implore you as aliens and strangers and exiles [*in this world*] to abstain from the sensual urges (the evil desires, the passions of the flesh, your lower nature) that wage war against the soul. Conduct yourselves properly (honorably, right-

Among the Gentiles, so that, although they may slander you as evildoers, [*yet*] they may by witnessing your good deeds [*come to*] glorify God in the day of inspection [*when God shall look upon you wanderers as a pastor or shepherd looks over his flock*]. Be submissive to every human institution and authority for the sake of the Lord, whether it be to the emperor as supreme, Or to governors as sent by him to bring vengeance (punishment, justice) to those who do wrong and to encourage those who do good service. For it is God's will and intention that by doing right [*your good and honest lives*] should silence (muzzle, gag) the ignorant charges and ill-informed criticisms of foolish persons. [*Live*] as free people, [*yet*] without employing your freedom as a pretext for wickedness; but [*live at all times*] as servants of God. Show respect for all men [*treat them honorably*]. Love the brotherhood (the Christian fraternity of which Christ is the Head). Reverence God. Honor the emperor. [*You who are*] household servants, be submissive to your masters with all [*proper*] respect, not only to those who are kind and considerate and reasonable, but also to those who are surly (overbearing, unjust, and crooked). For one is regarded favorably (is approved, acceptable, and thankworthy) if, as in the sight of God, he endures the pain of unjust suffering. [*After all*] what kind of glory [*is there in it*] if, when you do wrong and are punished for it, you take it patiently? But if you bear patiently with suffering [*which results*] when you do right and that is undeserved, it is acceptable and pleasing to God. For even to this were you called [*it is inseparable from your vocation*]. For Christ also suffered for you, leaving you [*His personal*] example, so that you should follow in His footsteps.

He personally bore our sins in His [*own*] body on the tree [*as on an altar and offered Himself on it*], that we might die (cease to exist) to sin and live to righteousness. By His wounds you have been healed. For you were going astray like [*so many*] sheep, but now you have come back to the Shepherd and Guardian (the Bishop) of your souls. [*Isa. 53:5, 6.*]

When we as true kingdom kings and priests begin to clean up our "act", and begin to both exemplify and preach the kingdom of God (teaching those things which concern the Lord Jesus Christ with all confidence, and truly celebrating his majesty, his power, and his greatness), the atmosphere will be set for signs and wonders to be done in his name; and with great power we'll give witness to the saving, redemptive, miracle working, delivering, and healing power of the Lord Jesus. And great grace will be upon us all to fulfill the Lord's purpose, and then...

All nations whom thou hast made shall come and worship before thee, O Lord; and shall glorify thy name. ∎

Psalms 86:9

Epilogue

> *I go to prepare a place for you…that where I am, there ye may be also.*
> *(John 14:2c & 3b)*

In John 14:2b Jesus proclaims these words:

> *I go to prepare a place for you.*
>
> *And if I go and prepare a place for you, I will come again, and receive you unto myself; that where I am, there ye may be also.*

It was no mere coincidence that the very first thing God instituted, after he created Adam, was a place where Adam could fellowship with him; a place of worship. And it is also no mere coincidence that the very place that Jesus went to prepare, was a place of eternal fellowship. He went to prepare a place where we (along with all the host of heaven) will be able to worship the Father throughout all eternity.

Rev 4:9-11

> *And when those beasts give glory and honor and thanks to him that sat on the throne, who liveth forever and ever, The four and twenty elders fall down before him that sat on the throne, and worship him that liveth forever and ever, and cast their crowns before the throne, saying, Thou art worthy, O Lord, to receive glory and honor and power: for thou hast created all things, and for thy pleasure they are and were created.*

Rev 5:11-14

> *And I beheld, and I heard the voice of many angels round about the throne and the beasts and the elders: and the number of them was ten thousand times ten thousand, and thousands of thousands; Saying with a loud voice, Worthy is the Lamb that was slain to receive power, and riches, and wisdom, and strength, and honor, and glory, and blessing. And every creature which is in heaven, and on the earth, and under the earth, and such as are in the sea, and all that are in them, heard I saying, Blessing, and honor, and glory, and power, be unto him that sitteth upon the throne, and unto the Lamb forever and ever. And the four beasts said, Amen. And the four and twenty elders fell down and worshipped him that liveth forever and ever.* ■

Worship the Lord in the beauty of holiness

(Psa 29:2b)

References & Resources

Sorge, Bob. *Exploring Worship: A Practical Guide To Praise & Worship.* Greenwood, Missouri: Oasis House 1987

Lascelle, Ruth Specter. *A Dwelling Place For God.* Van Nuys, California: Rock of Israel 1990

Munroe, Myles. *The Purpose & Power of Praise & Worship.* Shippensburg, Pennsylvania: Destiny Image 2000

Garlington, Joseph L. *Worship: The Pattern of Things in Heaven.* Shippensburg, Pennsylvania: Destiny Image 1997

Conner, Kevin. *The Tabernacle of David.* Portland, Oregon: Bible Temple - Conners Publictions 1976

Pink, Authur W. *The Life of David.* Grand Rapids, Michigan: Baker Book House 1998

HOLY SCRIPTURES

Exodus 19:6
And ye shall be unto me a kingdom of priests, and an holy nation.

Exodus 28:36-38a
And thou shalt make a plate of pure gold, and grave upon it, like the engravings of a signet, HOLINESS TO THE LORD. And thou shalt put it on a blue lace, that it may be upon the mitre; upon the forefront of the mitre it shall be. And it shall be upon Aaron's forehead.

1Peter 2:9
But ye are a chosen generation, a royal priesthood, an holy nation, a peculiar people; that ye should shew forth the praises of him who hath called you out of darkness into his marvelous light:

1Kings 8:10-11
And it came to pass, when the priests were come out of the holy place, that the cloud filled the house of the LORD, So that the priests could not stand to minister because of the cloud: for the glory of the LORD had filled the house of the LORD.

2Chronicles 5:11-14
And it came to pass, when the priests were come out of the holy place: ...Also the Levites which were the singers...with their sons and their brethren, being arrayed in white linen, having cymbals and psalteries and harps, stood at the east end of the altar, and with them an hundred and twenty priests sounding with trumpets... It came even to pass, as the trumpeters and singers were as one, to make one sound to be heard in praising and thanking the LORD; and when they lifted up their voice with the trumpets and cymbals and instruments of musick, and praised the LORD, saying, For he is good; for his mercy endureth for ever: that then the house was filled with a cloud, even the house of the LORD; So that the priests could not stand to minister by reason of the cloud: for the glory of the LORD had filled the house of God.

Psalms 111:1,6
I will praise the LORD with my whole heart, in the assembly of the upright, and in the congregation.

Psalm 107:32
Let them exalt him also in the congregation of the people, and praise him in the assembly of the elders.

Psalms 150:1-6
Praise ye the LORD. Praise God in his sanctuary: praise him in the firma--ment of his power. Praise him for his mighty acts: praise him according to his excellent greatness. Praise him with the sound of the trumpet; praise him with the psaltery and harp. Praise him with the timbrel and dance: praise him with stringed instruments and organs. Praise him up-on the loud cymbals: praise him upon the high sounding cymbals. Let everything that hath breath praise the LORD: Praise ye the Lord.

- NOTES -

The Cost Of Worship

www.ingramcontent.com/pod-product-compliance
Lightning Source LLC
Chambersburg PA
CBHW032059150426